COBAIN

By the Editors of Rolling Stone

Designed by Fred Woodward

Little, Brown and Company

BOSTON   NEW YORK   TORONTO   LONDON

A Rolling Stone Press Book

EDITOR Holly George-Warren
ASSISTANT EDITOR Shawn Dahl
DESIGNER Fred Woodward
DESIGN ASSOCIATE Fredrik Sundwall
PHOTO EDITOR Denise Sfraga

First Edition

ISBN 0-316-88034-5

Library of Congress Catalog
Card Number 94-78773

10 9 8 7 6 5

RRD-OH

Published simultaneously in Canada
by Little, Brown & Company (Canada)
Limited

Printed in the United States of America

A portion of the proceeds from
this book have been contributed to
the Kurt Cobain Scholarship Fund
(Aberdeen High School, 414 N. I St.,
Aberdeen, WA 98520)
and Cease-Fire Inc.
(1290 Avenue of the Americas,
New York, NY 10104).

n Cap Chew, Windowpane and Skid Row, before settling on Nirvana. **Spring 1987** The band plays their first gig at a house party in rural Raymond, Wash. They are nearly beaten up because they don't play any covers and they drink all their host's beer. **Fall 1987** Cobain moves from Aberdeen to Olympia, where he shares an apartment with his girlfriend, Tracy Marander. A few months later, he begins to experience a mysterious burning pain in his stomach. **Jan. 23, 1988** Nirvana records a 10-song demo tape in six hours with the godfather of grunge, legendary Seattle producer Jack Endino. Cobain pays the $152.44 for the session. Crover sits in on drums. Sub Pop co-honcho Jonathan Poneman hears the tape and offers to put out a Nirvana single. They accept. **Early Spring 1988** Burckhard is booted from Nirvana. His replacement, Dave Foster, lasts a matter of months. Burckhard rejoins and is quickly given the heave-ho again after he goes out on a beer run and manages to get Cobain's car impounded. **July 1988** Burckhard is replaced by Chad Channing, a drummer from affluent Bainbridge Island, across Puget Sound. **October 1988** A limited edition of 1,000 copies of the "Love Buzz"/"Big Cheese" single is released via Sub Pop's Singles Club. **Oct. 30, 1988** Cobain smashes his first guitar at a Halloween dorm party at Evergreen State University in Olympia. **March 1989** Influential British music weekly "Melody Maker" runs a series of pieces on the Seattle scene. The first grunge explosion is under way. **December 1988-January 1989** Nirvana begins putting down basic tracks for their debut album for Sub Pop with Jack Endino. The recording budget comes to a grand total of $606.17, paid for by Jason Everman, who joined the band soon afterward as second guitarist. **June 1989** "Bleach" is released on Sub Pop. The band embarks on a monthlong U.S. tour. Everman is booted from Nirvana at the end. **Oct. 20, 1989** Nirvana begins a six-week European tour with TAD. **December 1989** The "Blew" EP is released on Tupelo Records in the U.K. **April-May 1990** U.S. tour; at the end of the tour, Channing is boot-

Foreword

Denial. Anger. Depression. Guilt. Acceptance.
In the weeks following Kurt Cobain's death, the stages of grieving were manifested around ROLLING STONE. We especially stumbled through the fourth stage: guilt. As journalists, we had to pursue the story of Kurt Cobain's last days. As fans — Nirvana had revived our faith in rock & roll — we each just wanted to mourn his death in our own private way.

The editors of ROLLING STONE, after much discussion, decided that instead of rushing out a quick cover feature, an entire issue devoted to Cobain's story would be a fitting tribute. The thousands of letters from readers of ROLLING STONE's tribute issue told us we did the right thing.

When we decided to create a book commemorating the life and work of Kurt Cobain, we chose to expand upon the original issue. We've therefore included ROLLING STONE's first feature on Nirvana, stories on the band's sudden success and the Seattle music scene, and album and performance reviews. ROLLING STONE's last major interview with Kurt Cobain is also here as well as an extensive Q&A with Courtney Love, who was interviewed while on the Nirvana tour bus soon after Hole had finished recording "Live Through This." The majority of quotes appearing throughout the book were obtained in the days following Cobain's death by Alec Foege, who also contributed a critique of Nirvana's recorded legacy. Lorraine Ali's essay originally ran in the "New York Times," and Ann Powers' on-the-scene report appeared first in the "Village Voice." A time line, discography and tourography complete this book, our final tribute to Kurt Cobain and Nirvana.

1967

Cob

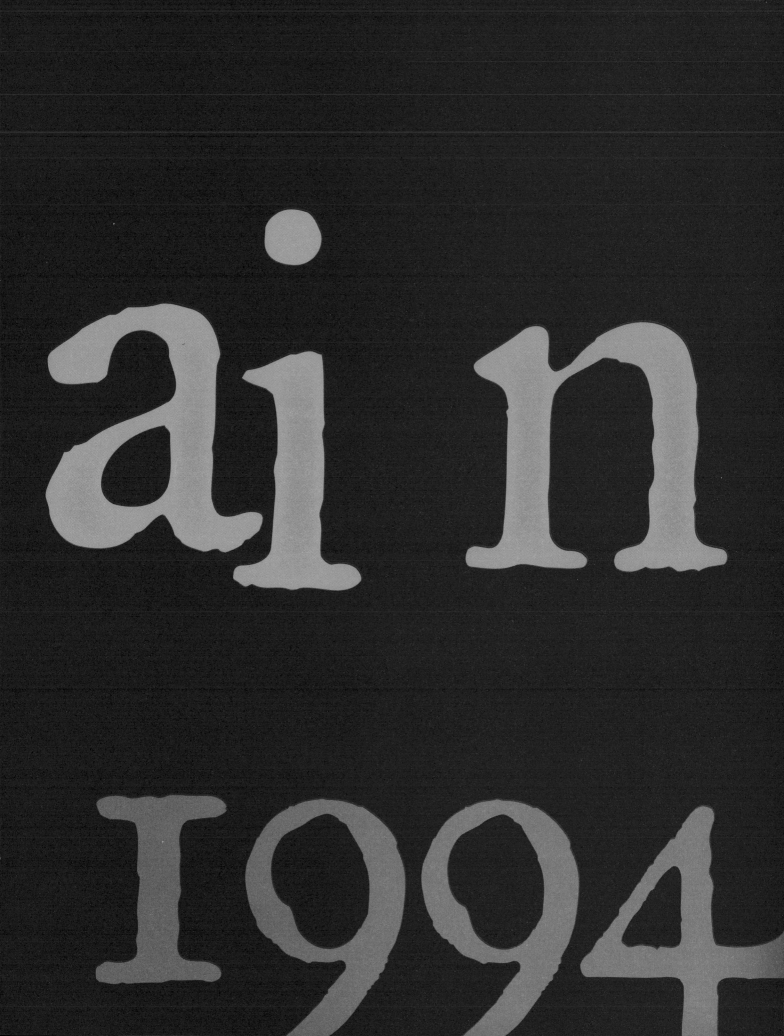

KURT COBAIN never wanted to be the spokesman for a generation, though that doesn't mean much: Anybody who did would never have become one. It is not a role you campaign for. It is thrust upon you, and you live with it. Or don't.

People looked to Kurt Cobain because his songs captured what they felt before they knew they felt it. Even his struggles — with fame, with drugs, with his identity — caught the generational drama of our time. Seeing himself since his boyhood as an outcast, he was stunned — and confused, and frightened, and repulsed, and, truth be told, not entirely disappointed (no one forms a band to remain anonymous) — to find himself a star. If Cobain staggered across the stage of rock stardom, seemed more willing to play the fool than the hero and took drugs more for relief than for pleasure, that was fine with his contemporaries. For people who came of age amid the greed, the designer-drug indulgence and the image-driven celebrity of the '80s, anyone who could make an easy peace with success was fatally suspect.

Whatever importance Cobain assumed as a symbol, however, one thing is certain: He and his band Nirvana announced the end of one rock & roll era and the start of another. In essence, Nirvana transformed the '80s into the '90s.

They didn't do it alone, of course — cultural change is never that simple. But in 1991, "Smells Like Teen Spirit" proved a defining moment in rock history. A political song that never mentions politics, an anthem whose lyrics can't be understood, a hugely popular hit that denounces commercialism, a collective shout of alienation, it was "(I Can't Get No) Satisfaction" for a new time and a new tribe of disaffected youth. It was a giant fuck-you, an immensely satisfying statement about the inability to be satisfied.

From that point on, Cobain battled to make sense of his new circumstances, to find a way to create rock & roll for a mass audience and still uphold his own version of integrity. The pressure of that effort deepened the wounds he had borne since boyhood: the broken home, the bitter resentment of the local toughs who bullied him, the excruciating stomach pains. He sought purpose in fatherhood. He wanted to soothe in his daughter, Frances Bean, his own primal fears of abandonment. He managed, finally, only to perpetuate them.

Cobain's life and music — his passion, his charm, his vision — can be understood and appreciated. His death leaves a far more savage legacy, one that will take many years to untangle. His suicide note

and Courtney Love's reading of it say it all. In his last written statement Cobain reels from cracked-actor posturing ("I haven't felt the excitement . . . for too many years now") to detached self-criticism ("I must be one of those narcissists who only appreciate things when they're gone") to self-pity ("I'm too sensitive") to a bizarre brand of hostile, self-loathing gratitude ("Thank you all from the pit of my burning, nauseous stomach") to, of all things, rock-star clichés ("It's better to burn out than to fade away").

Left with that, Love careens from reverence ("I feel so honored to be near him") to pained confusion ("I don't know what happened") to exasperation ("He's such an asshole") to anger ("Well, Kurt, so fucking what? Then don't be a rock star") to sobbing, heartbreaking guilt ("I'm really sorry, you guys. I don't know what I could have done").

No answers are forthcoming, because there are none. Suicide is an unanswerable act. It is said to be the one unforgivable sin, though our age has sought to forgive it by explaining it away in psychological or chemical terms. Earlier eras were not so kind. Suicides were buried at the crossroads. The message was severe: "You were at an impasse in your life and lacked the faith to make your way through it. Our lives are no easier to bear than yours. We may fall, but you chose to fall. We will make our way over you down the road of our destiny."

But suicide sends its own remorseless message. True, it is the ultimate cry of desperation, more harrowing than any scream Cobain unleashed in any of Nirvana's songs. True, he was in agony and saw no other way to end it. But suicide is also an act of anger, a fierce indictment of the living. If the inability to live is "sensitive," the ability to live comes to seem crass. "You're so good at getting over," the final message runs. "Get over this."

At 27, Kurt Cobain wanted to disappear, to erase himself, to become nothing. That his suicide so utterly lacked ambivalence is its most terrifying aspect. It all comes down to a stillness at the end of a long chaos: a young man sitting alone in a room, looking out a window onto Lake Washington, getting high, writing his goodbyes, pulling a trigger. You can imagine the silence shattering and then collecting itself, in the way that water breaks for and then envelops a diver, absorbing forever the life of Kurt Cobain.

--- ANTHONY DECURTIS

"In the last few weeks I was talking to Kurt a lot. We had a musical project in the works, but nothing was recorded. He loved Courtney and Frances Bean, and he loved Krist and Dave and Nirvana. He really loved those guys. His death is a profound loss, and I just don't think I can say anything else right now."

--- Michael Stipe *lead singer,* R.E.M.

BLEACH

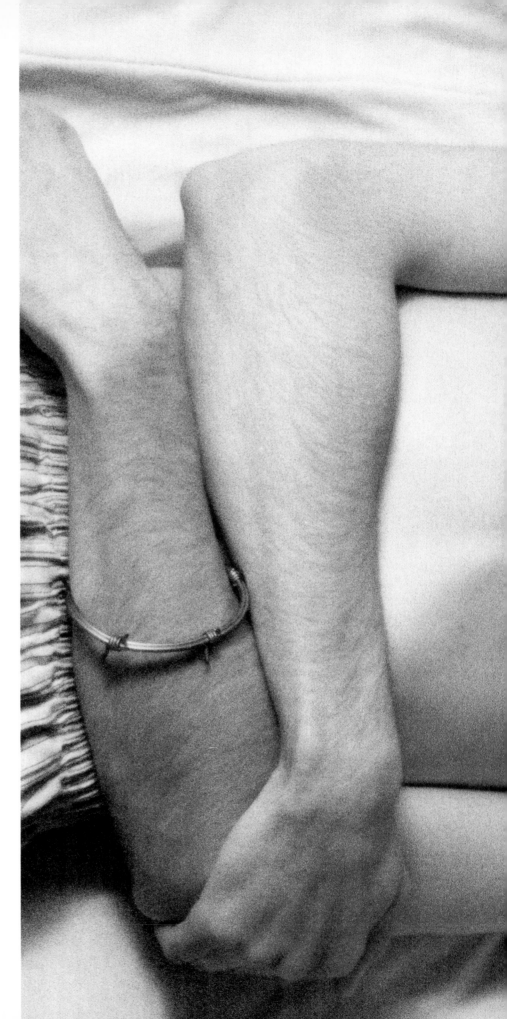

W HEN NIRVANA'S "BLEACH" was first released in 1989, it made plenty of noise. The trouble is, for all its scratching and clawing, the bludgeoning heavy metal and menacing punk rock, barely anyone heard the band's screams.

In light of the musical revolution ushered in by *Nevermind*, just two years later, the most remarkable aspect of *Bleach* might seem to be the fact that it was never reviewed in the first place. That, however, would not do justice to a debut that still holds up as a triumph of focused musical aggression, even in the post-*Nevermind* universe.

Despite sludgy production (the entire record cost only $606.17), *Bleach* kicks and screams with remarkable precision. "School" – which ends with Cobain repeatedly shrieking, "No recess" – is pure antisocial assault, while "Negative Creep," a mouthful of bile that spits out the words "I'm a negative creep and I'm stoned," proves, once and for all, that anger truly can be power.

What ultimately makes *Bleach* a cut above most albums' ranting is the glimpse at Cobain's growing pop genius. "About a Girl," an almost-whispered three minutes of sing-along heaven, is as pure a songwriting moment as anything that would follow it in the Cobain canon. Toss in "Love Buzz" – the cover of a hit by the Swedish band Shocking Blue that was Nirvana's first-ever Sub Pop single – and it's immediately clear that the group's later schlock-pop allegiances were not simply affectations.

Sure, Cobain's lyric-writing skills were less than fully developed. There is very little insight to be offered by songs like "Floyd the Barber" or "Blew," but who cares? Who really knew what the hell he was saying in "Smells Like Teen Spirit" anyway? With Nirvana, the medium is the message, and *Bleach* is a frighteningly wonderful introduction to their world.

--- CHRIS MUNDY

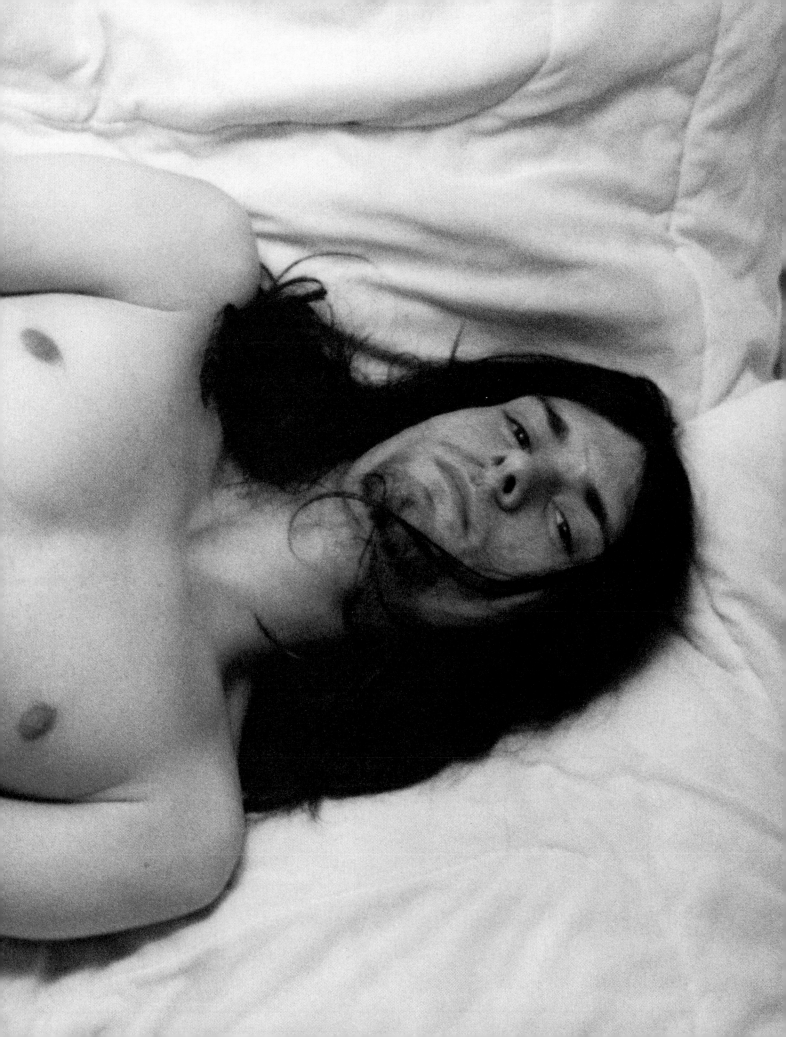

'He was an amazing guy, he was a complete gentleman. A goodhearted guy. He was one of those people --- everybody's got them in their life --- somebody that you turn to when things aren't going so good.'

--- MARK LANEGAN, lead singer, Screaming Trees

NEVERMIND

In late August 1991, I was a reporter for "Rolling Stone" at K Records' International Pop Underground convention (IPU) in Olympia, Wash., where such newcomers as Tsunami, Bikini Kill and 7 Year Bitch were joining Fugazi, Beat Happening, Melvins, Jad Fair, L7 and other big-scene names to reshape the future of indie rock. Besides unanimous agreement that a wonderful time was being had, the town was buzzing about advance tapes of the forthcoming Nirvana album.

Like many others, I had been bewildered as to why Geffen paid a lot of money to sign a group with one nothing-special punk album on Sub Pop. But the word was that Kurt Cobain had woodshedded a batch of catchy pop tunes and that the record was really good. Eager to hear the thing myself, I was thrilled to find a pre-release cassette in my mailbox when I got back to New York. "Nevermind" was indeed a great leap forward, but even the K-Fest afterglow couldn't alter the unavoidable reality that punk records were doomed to the far reaches of college-radio success, regardless of Geffen's largess or the idyllic faith of the band's fans.

It took some concerted pitching to place a "Nevermind" album review in "Rolling Stone," and the critique I wrote included a pre-emptive acknowledgment of its commercial futility (plus an erroneous acknowledgment of subsequently corrected dubbing errors on the advance cassette and no awareness of the CD's hidden track). History, of course, proved otherwise; in the two months that elapsed between submitting the review a week before the Sept. 24 release of "Nevermind" and its publication, the album was already well on its way to forever changing the music world. The IPU was right for the wrong reasons, and my faulty commercial prognostication underlined why some people are not meant to work for record companies.

DESPITE THE HAND-WRINGing the fanzines do each time an indie-rock hero signs a major-label deal, righteous postpunk stars from Hüsker Dü to Soundgarden have joined the corporate world without debasing their music. More often than not, ambitious left-of-the-dial bands gallantly cling to their principles as they plunge into the depths of commercial failure. Integrity is a heavy burden for those trying to scale the charts.

Led by singer-guitarist Kurt Cobain, Nirvana is the latest underground bonus baby to test mainstream tolerance for alternative music. Given the small corner of public taste that non-metal guitar rock now commands, the Washington State trio's version of the truth is probably as credible as anyone's. A dynamic mix of sizzling power chords, manic energy and sonic restraint, Nirvana erects sturdy melodic structures — sing-along hard rock as defined by groups like the Replacements, Pixies and Sonic Youth — but then attacks them with frenzied screaming and guitar havoc. When Cobain revs into high punk gear, shifting his versatile voice from quiet caress to raw-throated fury, the decisive control of bassist Krist Novoselic and drummer Dave Grohl is all that keeps the songs from chaos. If Nirvana isn't onto anything altogether new, *Nevermind* does possess the songs, character and confident spirit to be much more than a reformulation of college radio's high-octane hits.

Nirvana's 1989 debut, *Bleach*, relied on warmed-over '70s metal riffs, but *Nevermind* boasts an adrenalized pop heart and superior material, captured with roaring clarity by co-producer Butch Vig. Cued in with occasional (and presumably intentional) tape errors, most of the songs — like "On a Plain," "Come As You Are" and "Territorial Pissings" — exemplify the band's skill at inscribing subtlety onto dense, noisy rock. At the album's stylistic extremes, "Something in the Way" floats a translucent cloud of acoustic guitar and cello, while "Breed" and "Stay Away" race flat out, the latter ending in an awesome meltdown rumble.

Too often, underground bands squander their spunk on records they're not ready to make, then burn out their energy and inspiration with uphill touring. *Nevermind* finds Nirvana at the crossroads — scrappy garageland warriors setting their sights on a land of giants.

--- IRA ROBBINS

a vs. Fame

[January 23rd, 1992]

BLOOD IS POURING onto the floor of Nirvana's dressing room. To make matters worse, the source of the bleeding — a fan with a hole in his mouth where his front tooth used to be — has gone into shock and is convulsing uncontrollably.

Only a few minutes earlier, he was just one in a stupefied throng of 900 fans in Ghent, Belgium, fanatically watching the carnage. Nirvana lead singer/guitarist/instigator Kurt Cobain followed a headfirst dive into the crowd by clawing his way back onstage and systematically spitting on members of the audience standing in the first three rows. Bassist Krist Novoselic pulled a Perry Farrell-style full-frontal strip before trading places with drummer Dave Grohl, who played the bass while lying on his back in the middle of the stage. Cobain then took violent offense with the drums, wielding his guitar like an ax and splintering the kit like firewood. Next stop, a Marshall amp, which Cobain stabbed repeatedly with the guitar neck before he and Novoselic put the finishing touches on their instruments by smashing them together five times, the final impact shattering the bass and sending hunks

By Chris Mundy

of lumber into the crowd, striking the aforementioned fan flush in the face. The show, at this point, was over, Nirvana having done nothing if not put danger back into rock & roll. Cash from chaos. Never mind the Sex Pistols . . . Oh, well, whatever, never mind.

Backstage, Novoselic is kneeling next to the convulsing fan, trying to console him, as paramedics strap him to a chair and wheel him away. The band's tour manager is shrieking about finding equipment for the rest of the tour. Grohl has walked back into the empty hall, found the dislodged tooth, intact, in front of the stage and is making plans to turn it into a piece of jewelry. And Cobain is wandering through the wreckage. "Hey, everybody," he says repeatedly. "Why so glum?"

XPLOSIONS OF ALL SIZES have followed Nirvana, the most monstrous being the clamor over the band's latest offering, *Nevermind*. The follow-up to a striking Sub Pop debut album, *Bleach*, the trio's major-label coming-out is simultaneously the year's most passionate release and startling success story. A relentless barrage of thundering, fuck-you grunge-pop anthems, *Nevermind* has already sold over a million and a half copies since DGC Record's initial shipment of only 50,000 records on Sept. 24. But along with the overnight rise from the Seattle underground has come intense media scrutiny, pressure and, in turn, minor detonations like the Belgium show.

"That was the low point of the tour," says Novoselic two days later in Amsterdam. "It wasn't rock-star posing. A lot of what happened had to do with alcohol and with some really weird tension in the air. The whole course of events just couldn't be stopped. We were just on the train, and wherever it took us, we went. We're dealing with an extreme business here, so reactions are extreme."

Extreme records, it turns out, also spring forth from extreme individuals, and for Nirvana the world is seen through the eyes of Cobain, whose misanthropic view seems to inspire his remarkable gift. While Grohl handles road pressures with laid-back ease and Novoselic continually interjects a skewed sense of humor, Cobain rarely speaks to anyone surrounding him, usually curling up and turning his back to a crowd or mutely staring with the frightening intensity of a cornered animal. Having already shunned the *New York Times* and the *Los Angeles Times*, he at first refused to be interviewed for this article, changed his mind, then failed to surface two other times, in one instance hiding in a locked hotel room.

"When I joined the band, I lived with Kurt for eight months," says Grohl, 22. "When I first got there, he had just broken up with a girl and was totally heartbroken. We would sit in his tiny shoebox apartment for eight hours at a time without saying a word. For weeks and weeks this happened. Finally one night, we were driving back in the van, and Kurt said, 'You know, I'm not always like this.' And I just went, 'Whewww.'"

Raised by his mother, Cobain, 24, grew up in a trailer park in the redneck logging community of Aberdeen, Wash., about a hundred miles from Seattle, where, he has said, he never had a childhood

friend and steadily developed a hatred for the macho, guns-and-booze posturing around him. By the time he and Novoselic, 26, joined forces in 1987, borrowing a PA and four-track recorder from Cobain's aunt, the silent mistrust and pure punk ethic were firmly rooted. "The most anti-authority guy in the band is Kurt," says Novoselic. "The most anti-authority guy I *know* is Kurt. He'll be the one to walk up to people and scream, 'Why? Why? Why?' A lot of times I'll understand the reason behind things, even if I don't agree with it. Kurt's the guy out there yelling at the top of his lungs."

Focused frustration and blind rage come through loud and clear on *Nevermind*. Vacillating from being shimmery and hypnotic to being brutally assaultive, the songs are brief flashes of violence and retreat — classic pop shrouded in amplified fuzz and elements of danger. If guitars could talk, Cobain's would scream, melodically and irreverently, "What are you looking at?" And Grohl — who, as the group's fifth drummer, has finally given the band the propulsion it has always promised — bludgeons his drums as if they owe him money. Grohl, who had previously played with the Washington, D.C., hardcore heroes in Scream, has helped solidify the band's dynamic despite growing up far from the Seattle scene.

"Before I auditioned for the band, I talked to them on the phone, but I'd never met them," says Grohl. "I'd seen them once backstage at a Melvins show, and I found them quite amusing. There was Krist, this big, tall guy, jumping all around, and then there was Kurt, sitting in the corner like he was taking a shit. He was sitting there, legs crossed, not even looking at anybody."

With Grohl in place and two years of gigs between *Bleach* and *Nevermind*, the startling collection of songs for the new album began taking shape. The entire disc cashes in on the promise of *Bleach* and the fantastic single "Sliver." *Nevermind* careens through Cobain's world, from the subdued, then violent wail of "Lithium" to "Polly," the unnervingly stark acoustic rendering of a rapist tormenting his victim. More than sounding like us vs. them, *Nevermind* sounds like *me* vs. *you*. "A big factor has been a lot of political and social discontent," says Novoselic. "When we went to make this record, I had *such* a feeling of us vs. them. All those people waving the flag and being brainwashed, I really hated them. And all of a sudden, they're all buying our record, and I just think, 'You don't get it at all.'"

Yet another misunderstanding surrounding Nirvana is that the band plays, or even embraces, heavy metal — a myth perpetuated by reams of rave reviews from metal mags and an appearance on MTV's *Headbangers Ball*, for which Cobain arrived wearing a dress, stating, "I'm dressed for the ball."

"Metal's searching for an identity because it's exhausted itself, so they're going to latch onto us," says Novoselic. "We're not metal fans. There's a lack of insight into anything on a higher level." Grohl agrees. "It's the attitude that sets it apart," he says. "When you think of heavy metal, you think of sexist innuendoes and pseudo-Satanism." Novoselic concurs. "A lot of heavy-metal kids are just plain dumb," he says. "I'm sorry. We're heavy, but we're not heavy metal."

Nirvana's roots can be fairly easily traced to a stormy marriage of punk and pop. All three members are unabashed about admitting to pop childhoods (the CD of choice on the Nirvana tour bus is *Abba's Greatest Hits*), and all would be quick to tell you that strains of their music can be traced back to Liverpool. "When it comes down to pop, there's only one word – the *B* word," says Grohl. "Beatles. We might as well just play fucking Beatles covers for the rest of our careers." Says Novoselic, "They started it, they did it best, they ended it."

But while *Nevermind* nods at the melody of pop past, it's not likely that many Top 40 hits will contain squalls of feedback or a singer screaming as if he's exorcising a lifetime of demons. And it's less likely that a check of the charts will reveal titles like "Territorial Pissings" and "Drain You" or a song featuring Cobain shrieking: "I'm a negative creep, and I'm stoned" (from *Bleach*'s "Negative Creep"). In the melt and marriage of their influences, Nirvana comes off sounding like the Sweet fronted by Jeffrey Dahmer.

The personalities of the two albums – *Nevermind*'s blistering tunefulness and *Bleach*'s menacing immediacy – stem, in part, from the reality of the band's surroundings. "*Bleach* was recorded for [about] $600 on eight tracks," says Novoselic. "We recorded in three days, hacked it in, hacked it out. The sense of urgency shows through. On *Nevermind*, we were lucky to record in this studio from the '70s. It was like a time machine. It was like an old pair of corduroys that was starting to wear out. Just like a studio Abba would have recorded in. We'd just stagger in late, then get intense with it."

The staggering intensity of public reaction, however, has thrown Nirvana into a tailspin. The band has been deluged with interview requests and promotional appearances, making band life a 24-hour-a-day job. At an Amsterdam radio appearance, the production crew requested a gaggle of tunes from *Nevermind*. Without responding, the band played a Leadbelly cover and composed a new song on air, Cobain stopping at the beginning to say: "Wait a minute. I have to think of some words for this." Outdistancing the likes of Guns n' Roses, Mariah Carey, Michael Bolton and Metallica on the *Billboard* charts, it seems, has cast overwhelming shadows of doubt over Nirvana's self-image as underground, anti-mainstream operatives.

"We wanted to do as good as Sonic Youth," says Novoselic. "We totally respect those people and what they've done. We thought we'd sell a couple hundred thousand records at the most, and that would be fine. Next thing you know, we go Top 10. I wish we could have a time machine and go back to two months ago. I'd tell people to get lost." Grohl echoes the fact that Sonic Youth – for whom Nirvana was opening just a few short months ago – is the band's measuring stick for integrity. "We can relate to Sonic Youth because we're from the same school," says Grohl. "People ask us why they didn't sell 500,000 records, and my only answer is that people are fucking stupid."

So, the good and bad news for Nirvana is that it is the first of the slew of indie bands that made the jump to a major label – from Sonic Youth to Dinosaur Jr to Firehose – to triumph in the mainstream, in large part due to the fact that it is the first band to deliver the goods. At a critical juncture of rock's resurgence, hard rock and metal have garnered mass appeal but are no longer unnerving. Nirvana delivers intimidation in spades. From the video images of Cobain snarling to the album's out-of-focus inside photo of his giving the finger – telling everyone who buys his record to fuck themselves – Nirvana has taken fans to an edge they seldom inch toward. And at the same time, the songs are familiar enough to

offer an air of safety, however uneasy, that other bands can't provide. You can actually *hum* the damn things.

The band hopes that once it has leapt into the mainstream, it might just gain the opportunity to subvert from within. "Our justification for all the attention we're getting is that, maybe, a lot of other underground bands will get noticed," says Novoselic. "That's the only way we can deal with it."

The band members' main dissatisfaction with their public portrayal is the media depiction of them as rock brats simply mirroring the nihilism they rail against, rather than concentrating on their sincere efforts to focus attention on such problems as sexism and repression. "There's this saying, 'What's the value of preaching if man isn't redeemable?' " says Novoselic. "I go back and forth on that, but basically we're total optimists. We don't have any agenda. We can yell, 'Revolution,' and we can yell, 'The middle class is fucked – go down and smash all the windows.' But then what? There's no agenda. All we are saying is 'Be aware.' There's a lot of information out there. Use it."

Then again, this *is* still a band that got kicked out of its own record-release party. "No one wants to be under someone else's control," says Grohl, before Novoselic jumps in quickly. "It's, like, I have this hash, and I'm going to have to give it away when we leave Amsterdam," he says. "There's nothing wrong with it. I'm not going to hurt anybody. Authority and the whole policeman mentality is just fucked. I've been arrested before. I've had police come to my house. So many cops are just dumb."

Now, as *Nevermind* remains rooted in rock's elite Top 10 and the video for its first single "Smells Like Teen Spirit," continues to log hours and hours of MTV airplay, the band remains slightly blinded by the spotlight and amused the single's revulsion of teen apathy is being construed as a youthful call to arms. "I'm looking forward to being older," says Novoselic. "I've got everything going against youth that I possibly can. I'm married. I'm losing hair. I heard somebody say that Nirvana is against the old generation. That's not right. We're just against that old guard."

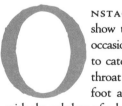

NSTAGE IN AMSTERDAM, with the Belgium show two days forgotten, Nirvana is relentless – occasionally giving the hysterical crowd a chance to catch its breath just before punching it in the throat again. Novoselic bobs up and down barefoot across the stage as Grohl clubs his drums with the subtlety of a boot to the groin. Cobain, regular guitar out of commission, sports one with a sticker that reads VANDALISM: BEAUTIFUL AS A ROCK IN A COP'S FACE as he dives at a cameraman who is trying to film from the edge of the stage. The only explosion tonight is Nirvana erupting into the fiercest set in rock & roll, Cobain shrieking the final lines of "Territorial Pissings," the band's bile-spewing antisexism rant, and then leaping over the drums, into Grohl's arms, to be carried offstage. End of show. End of story. Enough said. "Any good review," says Grohl, "should just say, 'They got up onstage, they played 15 songs, and they left. It was loud. People were slam-dancing. I went home with a headache. Nirvana.' What more is there to say?" ◐

Inside *the* Heart & Mind *of* Nirvana

By Michael Azerrad

FOR NOW, Kurt Cobain and his new wife, Courtney Love, live in an apartment in Los Angeles' modest Fairfax District. The living room holds little besides a Fender Twin Reverb amplifier, a stringless guitar, a makeshift Buddhist shrine and the couple's collection of naked plastic dolls.

Scores of CDs and tapes are strewn around the stereo — obscurities such as Calamity Jane, Cosmic Psychos and Billy Childish, as well as Cheap Trick and the Beatles. "Norwegian Wood" drifts down the hall to the dimly lit bedroom, where Cobain lies flat on his back in pajamas, a red-painted big toenail peeking out the other end of the blanket and a couple of teddy bears lying beside him for company. The surprisingly fragrant L.A. night seeps through the window screen.

He's been suffering from a longstanding and painful stomach condition — perhaps an ulcer — aggravated by stress and, apparently, his screaming singing style. Having eaten virtually nothing for over two weeks, Cobain, 25, is strikingly gaunt and frail, far from the stubbly doughboy who smirked out from a photo inside *Nevermind*. It's hard to believe this is the same guy who smashes guitars and wails with such violence — until you notice his blazing blue eyes and the faded pink and purple streaks in his hair.

Cobain had abruptly canceled an earlier interview, partly because of the anti-Nirvana letters that recently dominated ROLLING STONE's Correspondence page and partly because the magazine borrowed the title of the band's hit single "Smells Like Teen Spirit" for a headline on the recent *Beverly Hills, 90210* cover.

Then he came around. "There are a lot of things about ROLLING STONE that I've never agreed with," says Cobain in a gentle growl one or two steps up from a whisper. "But it's just so old school to fight amongst your peers or people that are dealing with rock & roll, whether or not they're dealing with it in the same context that you would like to. There are a lot of political articles in there that I've been thankful for, so it's really stupid to attack something that you're not 100 percent opposed to. If there's a glimmer of hope in anything, you should support it.

"I don't blame the average 17-year-old punk-rock kid for calling me a sellout," Cobain adds. "I understand that. Maybe when they grow up a little bit, they'll realize there's more things to life than living out your rock & roll identity so righteously."

"ALL I NEED IS A BREAK, and my stress will be over with," says Cobain. "I'm going to get healthy and start over."

He's certainly earned a break after playing nearly 100 dates on four continents in five months, never staying in one place long enough for a doctor to tend to his stomach problem. And he and his band mates, bassist Krist Novoselic and drummer Dave Grohl, have had to cope with the peculiar position of being the world's first triple-platinum punk-rock band.

Soon after the September release of *Nevermind*, MTV pumped "Teen Spirit" night and day as the album vaulted up the charts until it hit No. 1. Although the band's label, DGC, doubted the album would sell over 250,0000 copies, it sold 3 million in just four

months and continues to sell nearly 100,000 copies a week.

For Nirvana, putting out their first major-label record was like getting into a new car. But the runaway success was like suddenly discovering that the car was a Ferrari and the accelerator pedal was Krazy Glued to the floorboard. Friends worried about how the band was dealing with it all.

"Dave's just psyched," says Nils Bernstein, a good friend of the band members' who coordinates their fan mail. "He's 22, and he's a womanizer, and he's just: '*Score!*'" Novoselic, according to Bernstein, had a drinking problem but went on the wagon this year.

But rumors are flying about Cobain. A recent item in the music-industry magazine *Hits* said Cobain was "slam dancing with Mr. Brownstone," Guns n' Roses slang for doing heroin. A January profile in *BAM* magazine claimed that Cobain was "nodding off in mid-sentence," adding "the pinned pupils, sunken cheeks and scabbed, sallow skin suggest something more serious than mere fatigue."

Cobain denies he is using heroin. "I don't even drink anymore because it destroys my stomach," he protests. "My body wouldn't allow me to take drugs if I wanted to, because I'm so weak. All drugs are a waste of time. They destroy your memory and your self-respect and everything that goes along with your self-esteem. They're no good at all. But I'm not going to go around preaching against it. It's your choice, but in my experience, I've found they're a waste of time."

Cobain brushes off speculation that he's finding fame difficult and dismisses rumors that he'll soon break up the band because it has become too big. "It really isn't affecting me as much as it seems like it is in interviews and the way that a lot of journalists have portrayed my attitude," he says. "I'm pretty relaxed with it."

But people who know him say otherwise. Choosing his words carefully, Jack Endino, producer of the band's debut album, *Bleach*, says, "When I saw them in Amsterdam a few months back, it seemed like they were a little grouchy and . . . under pressure."

Fame rubs against Cobain's punk ethos, which is why he refused a limo ride to Nirvana's *Saturday Night Live* appearance. "People are treating him like a god, and that pisses him off," says Bernstein. "They're giving Kurt this elevated sense of importance that he feels he doesn't have or deserve. So he's like 'Fuck you!' Krist and Dave have had to pick up a lot of Kurt's slack. Krist and Dave were close before, but now they're inseparable."

"Just to survive lately, I've become a lot more withdrawn from the band," Cobain confesses. "I don't go party after the show; I go straight to my hotel room and go to sleep and concentrate on eating in the morning. I'd rather deal with things like that. Our friendship isn't being jeopardized by it, but this tour has definitely taken some years off of our lives. I plan to make changes."

Stress has gotten to Cobain before. He had an onstage breakdown at a 1989 show in Rome, near the end of a particularly grueling European tour. Says Bruce Pavitt, co-owner of Sub Pop Records, Nirvana's first label: "After four or five songs, he quit playing and climbed up the speaker column and was going to jump off. The bouncers were freaking out, and everybody was just begging him to come down. And he was saying, 'No, no, I'm just going to dive.' He had really reached his limit. People literally saw a guy wig out in front of them who could break his neck if he didn't get it together." Cobain was eventually talked down.

If he can stand the heat, Cobain, extremely bright and unafraid to take provocative stands, may emerge as a John Lennon-like figure. The comparison with Cobain's idol isn't frivolous. Like Lennon, he's using his music to scream out an unhappy childhood. And like Lennon, he's deeply in love with an equally provocative and visionary artist – Courtney Love, leader of the fiery neo-feminist band Hole.

Cobain and Love were married on Feb. 24 in a secluded location in Waikiki, Hawaii, after Nirvana's tour of Japan and Australia, with only a female nondenominational minister and a roadie as a witness. "It's like Evian water and battery acid," Cobain said of the couple's chemistry. And when you mix the two? "You get love," says Cobain, smiling for the first time. Exhausted and bedridden, Cobain is still so smitten that he can proclaim: "I'm just happier than I've ever been. I finally found someone that I'm totally compatible with. It doesn't matter whether she's a male, female or hermaphrodite or a donkey. We're *compatible*." Whenever Love walks into the room, even if it's to scold him about something, he gets the profoundly dopey grin of the truly love struck.

"**I** HAVE THOUGHT ABOUT IT, and I can't come to any conclusions at all," says Cobain of *Nevermind*'s success. "I don't want to sound egotistical, but I know it's better than a majority of the commercial shit that's been crammed down people's throats for a long time."

Nevermind embodies a cultural moment; "Smells Like Teen Spirit" is an anthem for (or is it against?) the "Why Ask Why?" generation. Just don't call Cobain a spokesman for a generation. "I'm a spokesman for *myself*," he says. "It just so happens that there's a bunch of people that are concerned with what I have to say. I find that frightening at times because I'm just as confused as most people. I don't have the answers for anything. I don't want to be a fucking spokesperson."

"That ambiguity, that's the whole thing," says *Nevermind* producer Butch Vig. "What the kids are attracted to in the music is that he's *not* necessarily a spokesman for a generation, but all that's in the music – the passion and [the fact that] he doesn't necessarily know what he wants, but he's pissed. It's all these things working at different levels at once. I don't exactly know what 'Teen Spirit' means, but you know it means *something*, and it's intense as hell."

Cobain agrees the message isn't necessarily in the words. "Most of the music is really personal as far as the emotion and the experiences that I've had in my life," he says, dragging on a cigarette, "but most of the *themes* in the songs aren't that personal. They're more just stories from TV or books or movies or friends. But definitely the emotion and feeling is from me. "Most of the concentration of my singing is from my upper abdomen, that's where I scream, that's where I feel, that's where everything comes out of me – right here," he continues, touching a point just below his breastbone. It just happens to be exactly where his stomach pain is centered.

When *Nevermind* hit No. 1, Cobain was "kind of excited," he says. "I wouldn't admit that at the time. I just hope that it doesn't end with us. I hope there are other bands that can keep it going."

Although Cobain is thrilled when underground bands infiltrate the mainstream charts, he's outraged by others who are riding the coattails of the alternative boom. His favorite target is Pearl Jam, also from Seattle, which he accused of "corporate, alternative and cock-rock fusion" in a recent *Musician* magazine interview. "Every article I see written about them, they mention us, and they're baiting that fact," says Cobain, sitting up cross-legged on the bed. "I would love to be erased from my association with that band and other corporate bands like the Nymphs and a few other felons. I do feel a duty to warn the kids of false music that's claiming to be underground. They're jumping on the alternative bandwagon."

"I don't know what I did to him; if he has a personal vendetta against us, he should come to us," says Pearl Jam's Jeff Ament, who says Cobain barely even said hello when they did a recent minitour together. "To have that sort of pent-up frustration, the guy obviously must have some really deep insecurities about himself. Does he think we're riding his bandwagon? We could turn around and say that Nirvana put out records on money we made for Sub Pop when we were in Green River – if we were that stupid about it."

Cobain is happier to reel off a list of some of the bands he *does* like: the Breeders, Pixies, R.E.M., Jesus Lizard, Urge Overkill, Beat Happening, Dinosaur Jr and Flipper.

For the members of Nirvana, plugging fellow underground musicians is one of the few consolations for the pressures of fame. When the band played Seattle's Paramount Theater for its big homecoming show last Halloween, its opener was Bikini Kill, a confrontational female-led band from nearby Olympia that came out in lingerie with SLUT written across their stomachs.

Helping out alternative types strengthens the community that made Nirvana's success possible. "It's not a matter of destroying the music industry," explains Sub Pop co-owner Jonathan Poneman, "it's a question of being able to be *included*. Egalitarian revolution – that's what makes them a punk-rock band."

IT'S FITTING that Nirvana bumped Michael Jackson off the No. 1 spot on the pop charts. Cobain and Jackson have little in common – it doesn't matter if you're black or white, but when Cobain hears such saccharine platitudes, he screams. Jackson's music is '80s-style ear candy, while Nirvana makes grass-roots music for the '90s. There's no glamour in Nirvana, no glamour at all, in fact.

Novoselic and Cobain come from rural Aberdeen, Wash., a hundred miles southwest of Seattle, where Novoselic's mom runs Maria's Hair Design. Aberdeen has seen better days – namely, during the whaling era in the mid-19th century, when the town served as one big brothel for visiting sailors, a fact that Novoselic has said makes residents "a little ashamed of our roots." Pervasive unemployment and a perpetually rainy, gray climate have led to rampant alcoholism and a suicide rate more than twice the already high state average. The local pawnshop is full of guns, chain saws and guitars.

One of the more popular bars in town is actually called the Pourhouse, which is where two young men about Cobain's age, Joe and James, sit down for a pitcher of beer – each. Joe is out of work because his leg is broken. "I tried to fly off a house," he explains.

"Yeah, I know the Cobain kid," says James. "Faggot."

"He's a *faggot*?" asks Joe, taken aback. Recovering quickly, he declares: "We *deal* with faggots here. We run 'em out of town."

This is where Cobain and Novoselic grew up. That's why they kissed each other full on the lips as the *SNL* credits rolled. They knew it would piss off the folks back home — and everybody like them.

"I definitely have a problem with the average macho man — the strong-oxen working-class type," Cobain says wearily, "because they have always been a threat to me. I've had to deal with them most of my life — being taunted and beaten up by them in school, just having to be around them and be expected to be that kind of person when you grow up. I definitely feel closer to the feminine side of the human being than I do the male — or the American idea of what a male is supposed to be. Just watch a beer commercial, and you'll see what I mean."

Of course, Cobain was miserable in high school. Surrounded by metalheads whose only prospects were unemployment or risking life and limb hacking down beautiful centuries-old trees, Cobain was a sensitive sort, small for his age and uninterested in sports.

"As I got older," says Cobain, a fan of Beckett's, Burroughs', and Bukowski's, "I felt more and more alienated — I couldn't find friends whom I felt compatible with at all. Everyone was eventually going to become a logger, and I knew I wanted to do something different. I wanted to be some kind of artist."

"If he would have been anywhere else," says his mother, Wendy O'Connor, "he would have been fine — there would have been enough of his kind not to stick out so much. But this town is just exactly like *Peyton Place.* Everybody is watching every one and judging, and they have their little slots they like everyone to stay in — and he didn't."

A friend of Cobain's half-joked that *Nevermind* sold to every abused child in the country, and maybe that's not far from the truth — the divorce rate soared to nearly 50 percent in the mid-'70s, and all those children of broken homes are becoming adults. Including Kurt Cobain.

Cobain started life as a sunny child. "He got up every day with such joy that there was another day to be had," recalls his mother. "When we'd go downtown to the stores, he would sing to people." Cobain's intelligence was apparent early on. "It kind of scared me because he had perceptions like I've never seen a small child have," his mother continues. "He had life figured out really young. He knew life wasn't always fair. Kurt was focused on the world — he would be drawing in a coloring book, and the news would be on, and he was very attuned to that, and he was just three and a half."

"He had make-believe friends, too," O'Connor says. "There was one called Boddah — he blamed everything on him. He had to have a place at the table — it just became ridiculous. One day his Uncle Clark asked if he could take Boddah with him to Vietnam because he was lonely there. And Kurt took me aside and whispered in my ear: 'Boddah isn't real. Does Clark know that?'"

But Cobain's parents — a secretary and an auto mechanic — divorced when he was 8, and "it just destroyed his life," says his mother. "He changed completely. I think he was ashamed. And he became very inward — he just held everything in. He became real shy. It just devastated him. I think he's still suffering." A bit of a "juvenile," as he puts it, Cobain was shuffled from his mother to his father, uncles and grandparents and back again.

Cobain listened to nothing but the Beatles until he was 9, when his dad began subscribing to a record club and albums by Led Zeppelin, Kiss and Black Sabbath began arriving in the mail. Then Kurt began following the Sex Pistols' American tour in magazines. He didn't know what punk sounded like, because no store in town stocked the records, but he had an idea. "I was looking for something a lot heavier, yet melodic at the same time," Cobain says, "something different from heavy metal, a different attitude."

Cobain idolized the Aberdeen band the Melvins and drove their tour van, hauled their equipment and watched over 200 of their rehearsals, by his estimate. Melvins leader Buzz Osborne became his friend and mentor and took 16-year-old Cobain to his first rock show — Black Flag. According to erstwhile Melvins bassist Matt Lukin (now in Mudhoney), "He was totally blown away." It was about this time that Cobain moved from drums to guitar.

"I don't think he had a hell of a lot of friends," Lukin recalls. "He was always trying to start bands, but it was hard to find people who wouldn't flake out on him." Osborne introduced him to Novoselic, a shy youth so tall (he's six foot seven) that he bumped his head on the beams in Cobain's house. Cobain formed a band with this kindred spirit two years his senior. They went through names like Ed, Ted and Fred; Skid Row; and Fecal Matter before settling on Nirvana. Nerves and crummy equipment hampered their live attack, but Nirvana slowly developed a powerful sound, becoming very popular in neighboring Olympia, where they would play wild parties at Evergreen State College.

Meanwhile, Cobain's mother kicked him out of the house after he quit high school and played in bands instead of getting a job. Homeless, Cobain slept on friends' couches. At one point, he lived under a bridge in Aberdeen, an arrangement chronicled in *Nevermind*'s "Something in the Way."

A vandal with a cause, Cobain loved to spray-paint the word *queer* on four-by-four trucks, the redneck vehicle of choice. Other favorite graffiti included GOD IS GAY and ABORT CHRIST. In 1985 Novoselic, Osborne and 18-year-old Cobain wrote HOMOSEXUAL SEX RULES on the side of an Aberdeen bank (Osborne swears it said, QUIET RIOT). While Osborne and Novoselic hid in a garbage dumpster, Cobain was caught and arrested. A police report lists the contents of his pockets: a guitar pick, a key, a beer, a mood ring and a cassette by the militant punk band Millions of Dead Cops. He received a $180 fine and a 30-day suspended sentence.

"He is really a very angry person," says Sub Pop's Bruce Pavitt, "so he makes dramatic gestures that piss people off." But Cobain is also sensitive, and sensitive people are often the angriest. "Exactly," says Pavitt. "That's the key."

Cobain took jobs as a janitor at a hotel and at a dentist's office (where he dipped into the nitrous) and moved in with Matt Lukin, who was then with the Melvins. Just to freak the neighbors, Cobain made a satanic-looking doll and hung it from a noose in his window. He kept some pet turtles in a bathtub that he put in the front room. Then he realized there was no way to drain the water, so Lukin, a carpenter, simply cut a hole in the floor. The foundation eventually became waterlogged, leaving the rickety shack teetering.

In a demo session with producer Jack Endino, Cobain and Melvins drummer Dale Crover finished 10 songs in one afternoon. Impressed, Endino played the tape for Sub Pop's Jonathan Poneman. (Two cuts wound up on *Bleach.*)

At a Seattle coffee shop, Poneman met Cobain, who was awed by Sub Pop because it boasted one of his favorite bands, Soundgarden. Novoselic showed up a bit later. "Krist was drunk and belligerent," recalls Poneman, "and just didn't give a flying fuck about it – 'OK, you want to put out our records, that's cool.' And then he'd insult me." Poneman signed Nirvana anyway.

A year and two drummers later, in October 1988, Sub Pop released the single "Love Buzz"/"Big Cheese"; *Bleach* was released in June 1989, recorded for the princely sum of $606.17. (Jason Everman didn't actually play on the album, although he was credited as a guitarist because he bankrolled the recording. "We still owe him the $600," says Cobain. "Maybe I should send him off a check.")

Bleach sold slowly at first, but after a few months critical raves and effusive praise from indie kingpins Sonic Youth eventually helped *Bleach* to sell 35,000 copies, very impressive for an indie. (The album's sales exploded in the wake of *Nevermind*.)

But by this time, *Bleach* drummer Chad Channing was history. Osborne knew Dave Grohl from sharing bills with Grohl's band Scream. After Scream's bassist quit, Grohl called Osborne in desperation, and Osborne hooked him up with his old buddies in Nirvana. "Krist and Kurt liked Dave because he hits the drums harder than anybody," says producer Butch Vig.

In August 1990, Nirvana recorded six tracks with Vig for a planned Sub Pop album. *Bleach* was very good, but Cobain had returned to the studio with songs that were a quantum leap past anything he'd done before.

Meanwhile, Sub Pop had begun talking to major labels about a distribution deal. Figuring that if they had to be on a major label, they might as well choose it themselves, the members of Nirvana began shopping the Vig demos. Only a major could afford to buy Nirvana out of their Sub Pop contract, and major distribution would get their punk to the people. "That's pretty much my excuse for not feeling guilty about why I'm on a major label," says Cobain. "I should feel really guilty about it; I should be living out the old punk-rock threat and denying everything commercial and sticking in my own little world and not really making an impact on anyone other than the people who are already aware of what I'm complaining about. It's preaching to the converted."

A bidding war broke out among a handful of labels. Nirvana signed to DGC, the label run by entertainment magnate David Geffen, a subsidiary of giant MCA and the home of Guns n' Roses and Cher. The band received $287,000 in advance money.

The group approached R.E.M. producer Scott Litt and Southern pop maestro Don Dixon, but neither wound up taking the job, and the band chose Vig to produce instead. During rehearsals for the album, one song really stuck out. "As soon as they started playing 'Teen Spirit,'" Vig says, "it was awesome sounding. I was pacing around the room, trying not to jump up and down in ecstasy."

Nevermind was recorded last spring for $135,000, including living expenses, mastering and even Vig himself (he has since renegotiated his deal). Slayer producer Andy Wallace mixed the album. Vig knew something was up when all sorts of people started asking him for advance tapes; now he's besieged with offers to produce bands and "make them sound like Nirvana."

JUST LAST SEPTEMBER, Novoselic and Cobain were so poor they had to pawn their amps; now Cobain gets 20 bucks out of the cash machine and finds there's another $100,000 in his account. When Novoselic told a friend he'd bought a five-bedroom house in Seattle, the friend pointed out that payments would just be another headache. "What payments?" Novoselic replied. He'd paid for the house in full.

"A lot of people ask me: 'When's he going to buy you a new car? When's he going to buy you a house?'" says Cobain's mother. "I couldn't even accept it if he offered it. We could have helped him along if we would have realized that this was really going to be something. We thought he'd get over it. I wish we would have helped him out a little more. He owes us nothing."

Nirvana, however, owes DGC another record, which the band will likely start recording late this fall or early winter. Says Jonathan Poneman, "Either Kurt is going to create something that is an ornate masterpiece, or he is going to create something angry and filled with rage and confusion." Butch Vig thinks it might be a low-key acoustic album.

"I have a pretty good idea," says Cobain. "I think both of the extremes will be in the next album – it'll be more raw with some songs and more candy pop on some of the others. It won't be as one-dimensional."

One-dimensional or not, there's a good chance Cobain's audience just doesn't get his message. The antimacho "Territorial Pissings" was used as background music for a football show; "Smells Like Teen Spirit" might suffer the same fate as "Rockin' in the Free World" or "Born in the U.S.A." – listeners may not get the irony at all. Actually, Cobain called it in the chorus to *Nevermind*'s "In Bloom" – "He's the one who likes all the pretty songs/And he likes to sing along . . . /But he knows not what it means." Cleverly, the song is a natural-born sing-along, trapping listeners into the joke.

According to Nils Bernstein, most Nirvana fan letters are along the lines of "Hey, dude, I saw your video and bought your tape! You guys kick ass!"

"*Everybody* says, 'You guys kick *ass*,'" says Bernstein. About half ask for the lyrics to "Teen Spirit" (the complete lyrics to *Nevermind* will be included with the next single, "Lithium"). Most letter writers are between 10 and 22, buy cassettes and watch MTV. "There's not very many sexual letters," says Bernstein, "which is a drag. The ones from prison are the best ones; also the ones from the military." And what do soldiers say? "They say, 'Hey, you guys kick some *ass*!'"

Cobain accepts that much of his new audience is made up of the same types who hassled him in high school. "I can't have a lot of animosity toward them, because I understand that a lot of people's personalities aren't necessarily their choice – a lot of times, they're pushed into the way they live," he says. "Hopefully, they'll like our music and listen to something else that's in the same vein, that's a bit different from Van Halen. Hopefully, they'll be exposed to the underground by reading interviews with us. Knowing that we do come from a punk-rock world, maybe they'll look into that and change their ways a bit."

But it's doubtful that most of them ever will. "Yeah, it seems hopeless," Cobain says with a sigh. "But it's fun to fight. It gives you something to do. It relieves boredom." He laughs. ◖

39

C G

By Michæl
Azerrad

42

rUng e
t
V

"Everybody loves us/Everybody loves our town," sings Mudhoney's Mark Arm. "That's why I'm thinking of leaving it/Don't believe in it now…/It's so overblown."

With the spectacular success of Alice in Chains, Pearl Jam, Soundgarden and Nirvana, the Northwest music scene is a bona fide phenomenon, a success story in a nation starving to hear one.

Actually, Seattle really peaked back in 1989, when the bands that made its reputation were still in town. "The whole thing is happening all over again," says producer and Skin Yard guitarist Jack Endino. "And in a bizarre, self-parodied, too-big-for-life sort of way." Says Bruce Pavitt, co-owner of Seattle's Sub Pop Records: "There are no brakes on the hype at this point. It's just going through the roof."

In the past six years, Seattle has gone from a small but vibrant music scene to a rock mecca recently profiled by *Time*, *Entertainment Weekly* and *USA Today*. The Cameron Crowe film *Singles* stars Matt Dillon as a Seattle rocker who fronts a band called Citizen Dick — which includes members of Pearl Jam — with cameos by local rock-scene VIPs.

Overblown? Possibly. Over with? Definitely not.

4I

"**W**OW, THE NATIVES are restless tonight," exclaims Ron Nine of Love Battery during a brilliant set at Seattle's Off Ramp, where a wave of gleeful slam dancers has deposited yet another piece of human flotsam on the stage. When it comes to Seattle, the natives *are* restless — people they see every day can be members of their favorite band. And you couldn't make it nicer to go to a club — most feature excellent beers from the city's microbreweries, and admission rarely tops six bucks. The Off Ramp hands out free earplugs and serves up 50-cent plates of the mysterious "Hash After the Bash." Oh, and the bands are great. Welcome to Seattle, Rock City.

For major labels, the gold rush is on. Northwest bands are getting signed at the rate of one a week. Until recently, the Seattle scene seemingly reshuffled the same 30 or so musicians, but now scores of bands have moved to town, all competing for attention and club space. They come from places such as Los Angeles; Boise, Idaho; and Tucson, Ariz., whence the Supersuckers arrived three years ago. "There was no work in Tucson," says drummer Dan Siegel. "So you move where there's some work." "We're like a construction worker looking for a union," adds singer Eddie Spagetti.

THE SEATTLE PHENOMENON wouldn't have been possible without the network of college radio, fanzines and indie distributors that sprang up in the wake of punk rock; Minneapolis and Athens, Ga., established the viability of regional scenes. Seattle's repressive liquor laws stifled live music, but recording was cheap; in the mid-'80s, radio stations KCMU and KJET supported local bands, which were reviewed by the late *Backlash* and the Seattle *Rocket,* which remains the scene's respected commentator.

Mark Arm chalks it up to "the two *i*'s: isolation and inbreeding." Like Minneapolis, Seattle is a relatively isolated northern city with heavy precipitation and little to do except drink beer and jam in the basement; with the population barely topping half a million, everybody knows one another. While mid-'80s alternative bands were busy aping R.E.M. and the Replacements, Arm says, "there was this one corner of the map that was busy being really inbred and ripping off each other's ideas."

Free of major-label attentions, musicians just made music to please their friends. "It's not a cutthroat sort of thing," says Scott McCaughey of the Young Fresh Fellows. "It's more like 'Love Battery put out a cool single! Great, let's go see 'em!' Everybody's friends. It's not a competition thing."

In the early '80s any band that made it to Seattle stood to make a big impression, which is why the hard-touring bands on Southern California's blazing postpunk label SST — Hüsker Dü, Minutemen and Black Flag — became musical Johnny Appleseeds. Even Seattle's trademark hirsuter-than-thou look was inspired by the longhairs in Black Flag.

All this occurred in Seattle's thriving cultural environment, which boasts prominent art museums, an opera, a philharmonic and local luminaries such as Gus Van Sant, Matt Groening and Lynda Barry. A university town, Seattle is consistently rated one of the nation's most livable cities, and the low cost of living makes it easy to be in a band.

And of course, Sub Pop had a lot to do with it.

"Jon Poneman and Bruce Pavitt were the first people that ever told me that this scene was going to be huge," says Soundgarden's Chris Cornell. Poneman and Pavitt, both in their early 30s, are two extremely bright men who use words like *heretofore* and *détente* when discussing their music; still, Poneman can and does slam-dance with the best of 'em.

Sporting a degree in punk rock from freethinking Evergreen State College, Pavitt wrote an early-'80s fanzine called *Sub Pop* and began releasing cassette compilations of national indie stars, then he noticed something happening in his own back yard and released Green River's *Dry As a Bone.* In 1987, Poneman, an erstwhile KCMU DJ and local promoter, signed on to the new Sub Pop label after a mutual friend, Soundgarden's Kim Thayil, introduced him to Pavitt.

Modeling themselves on Motown Records and SST (and maybe a little Malcolm McLaren), Pavitt and Poneman created an alternative universe of stars such as Mudhoney, Soundgarden and Screaming Trees, not to mention Sub Pop itself. "Their marketing strategy has been to create Sub Pop as an identity," says *Rocket* managing editor Grant Alden, "to create trust that if it's on Sub Pop, it's worth owning, even if you've never heard of the band."

Documenting Seattle's then-obscure scene was 1988's epochal *Sub Pop 200,* a three-EP box set, complete with a 20-page booklet. The music could have fit onto one record, but Poneman and Pavitt wanted to make a statement. "It was just overkill — sheer overkill and maximum hype," says Pavitt.

Photographer Charles Peterson established the look for Sub Pop bands — all hair, sweat and guitars — while Jack Endino's raw production was the sound. In a word, it was grungy.

The costly but ingenious move of flying in a *Melody Maker* writer in 1989 panned out — the English press flipped, and in classic fashion, American A&R people soon rushed in, checkbooks at the ready. In a trice, Soundgarden, Screaming Trees, the Posies, Alice in Chains and others were snapped up.

Seattle became Grunge City. The music hailed '70s bands like Black Sabbath and Kiss, as well as proto-punks such as the Stooges, the MC5 and Blue Cheer. Endino calls grunge "'70s-influenced, slowed-down punk music," while Kim Thayil says it's "sloppy, smeary, staggering, drunken music." Poneman calls it "a backwoods yeti stomp."

In Seattle, where no one honks his horn, to make noise is to make a statement. "People want things to be pretty and gentle and soothing here," says Grant Alden. "And if you look at the world differently and you rebel against that, you end up sounding like Mudhoney." (There may be a chemical explanation, and no, it's not the water. By day, coffee-crazed Seattleites guzzle espresso in cafés on each corner; by night, they quaff oceans of beer — jolted by java and looped with liquor, no wonder the music sounds like it does.)

Noise has always figured in Northwest music. Named after the sonic booms of a nearby air-force base, Tacoma's Sonics — admired

42

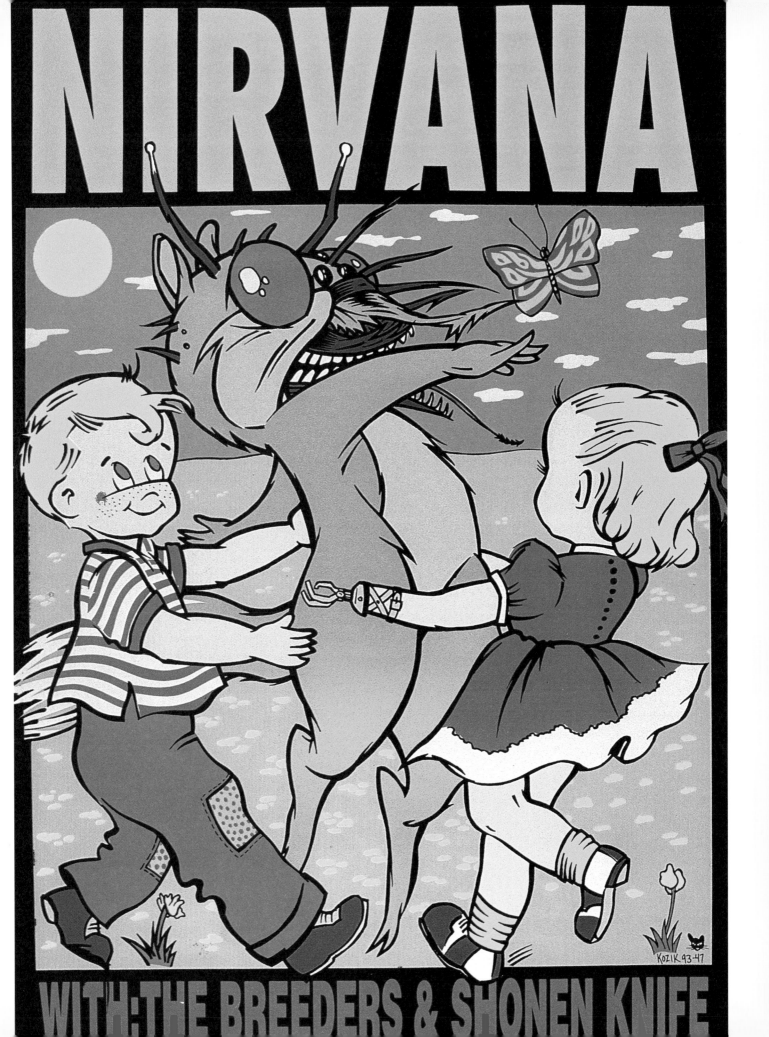

by everyone from Springsteen to the Sex Pistols – cut loose with bloodcurdling screams, Neanderthal drumming and heavily distorted guitar that sounded, well . . . grungy. And this was only 1964.

While the rest of America was mooning over Frankie and Fabian, Northwest kids were digging the Sonics, the Wailers and the Galaxies on the region's crazed teen-dance circuit. "Those bands have never been forgotten around here," says Scott McCaughey. "There was always a core of people who looked at that music as the Northwest tradition."

Paul Revere and the Raiders, the Kingsmen and the Ventures all came from the Northwest, where the original grunge classic, "Louie, Louie," first became a hit (and nearly became the state song in 1985). The region boasts many other illustrious native sons, from the doo-woppers the Fleetwoods to James Marshall Hendrix.

Typically, scores of punk bands popped up after a late-'70s Ramones gig at the elegant Olympic Hotel ballroom (there hasn't been a rock band there since). The scene bottomed out around '83, but then a new flock of bands, including the U-Men, Malfunkshun and the Melvins, started playing music that merged punk and metal, both the province of outsiders and outcasts; it was like someone putting their chocolate bar in someone else's peanut butter. Metal kids from Seattle's suburbs liked punk's exotic cool, while downtown punks liked metal for its theatricality, for its uncanny ability to annoy pointy-headed New Wavers and because it just plain rocked.

A tightknit core group emerged – the Melvins, Green River, Soundgarden and Malfunkshun. "We used to jam together a lot," says Cornell. "We talked about each other's bands, what we liked about 'em, what we hated about 'em. We talked about music a lot, we drank a lot."

The criminally overlooked Melvins virtually invented grunge simply by going from being the fastest band in town to being the slowest. "They got really heavy," recalls Mudhoney's Dan Peters, "and then a lot of bands decided they would be really heavy, too."

Malfunkshun bravely melded hardcore punk and the excesses of '70s glam rock. The band's Andy Wood ("a total star," says Cornell) hit even the tiniest stages in white face, glittery outfits and motorcycle boots with nailed-on platform heels and hollered, "Hellooooo, Seattle!" Green River's tense punk-metal fusion eventually snapped the band – "It was punk versus major-label deal," says former frontman Mark Arm. It is believed that the band's Jeff Ament was the first Seattle musician to proclaim he wanted to make music his living.

Green River's Ament, Stone Gossard and Bruce Fairweather joined Andy Wood to form Mother Love Bone and signed a major-money, major-label deal. Tragically, Wood died of a heroin overdose in early 1990, just weeks before the group's debut album was released. Polydor dropped the devastated band, but the Seattle rock community rallied around them, producing the moving memorial album *Temple of the Dog*, featuring Wood's onetime roommate Chris Cornell. Ament and Gossard later triumphed in Pearl Jam.

Although Wood's death raised awareness of the problem, heroin still runs rampant in Seattle. The Supersuckers' Eddie Spagetti says the band knows plenty of musicians who have experimented with the drug. "Most people come out of it saying, 'That's bad news,'" he says. "Or they die."

Privately, a number of sources confirm that several of Seattle's leading musical lights – members of internationally famous bands – are heroin users. The feeling around town is, the drug is a disaster waiting to happen.

On a lesser scale, last summer Sub Pop was a disaster that *was* happening. On the floor of its reception area is a sign that reads, YOU OWE DWARVES $. Last summer, the ribald psychopunkers weren't the only ones Sub Pop owed $ – back in August, the label was bouncing $100 checks.

For all of Pavitt and Poneman's smarts, they were no bean counters. They spent a small fortune pursuing an abortive deal with a major distributor (they won't say, but it was Sony), as well as coping with two costly copyright suits. Their fledgling distribution company had been hopelessly mismanaged, and they vainly tried to match the huge advances majors were now waving at local bands. Sub Pop began selling a T-shirt with its logo and the legend WHAT PART OF "WE HAVE NO MONEY" DON'T YOU UNDERSTAND? But thanks to restructuring their business, a lucrative Single of the Month Club and the best-selling album it had ever had, Mudhoney's *Every Good Boy Deserves Fudge*, Sub Pop gradually went into the black.

And then they *really* went into the black. Although Sub Pop rarely had contracts with its bands, Nirvana's Krist Novoselic went over to Pavitt's home one night, pounded drunkenly on his window and demanded one. Poneman wrote up a contract, which the band signed. When Nirvana signed to DGC, the label had to buy Sub Pop out of the band's two-album contract. Sub Pop got $75,000 and three points on each album sold. With *Nevermind* sales topping 3 million in the U.S. alone, that's $720,000 – so far. And Sub Pop nets an estimated $2.50 on each copy of Nirvana's first album, *Bleach*, which should go gold (500,000 copies) by the end of the year. But the best part of the deal might be the Sub Pop logo on every Nirvana disc.

S UB POP was still in the midst of its financial crisis when America's mightiest indie band finally decided to shop for a major, winding up with Warners. "We just kind of had it," says Mudhoney drummer Dan Peters. "We'd meet with them [Sub Pop], and they'd say, 'Come down tomorrow and we'll cut you a check.' And we'd go down there the next day, and they'd say, 'I didn't say that. You must have misunderstood me.'"

Mudhoney was the last of the original Seattle music community to graduate to the majors, a community that started to unravel when the bands began to go on lengthy national tours. "When you'd get back, the other band would be gone, and it wasn't the same thing anymore," Cornell says. Now the sniping begins: Mark Arm wrote the corrosive "Overblown" after seeing Soundgarden's bombastic video for "Outshined"; Nirvana and Pearl Jam are feuding after Kurt Cobain, in an interview, accused the band of selling out.

"The bands that created the scene are the bands that are out there getting the benefits of what they created," says Cornell. "And what's come in after that was never a scene to begin with. This scene was basically bound to end one way or another, and it's a happy ending in that the bands that started it are all having some good success." ●

Butthole Surfers
TAD NIRVANA
SEATTLE Center Arena
FRI 7 SAT 8 JANUARY
STARTS

"I don't think any of us would be in this room tonight if it weren't for Kurt Cobain,"

E dᵥd.ēd.dēer

to a capacity audience during a Washington D.C., concert the night Cobain's death was announced

New Noise for '93

AFTER A SUCCESSFUL European summer tour and a sold-out show at the mammoth 45,000-seat Velez Sarsfield Stadium, in Buenos Aires, Argentina, what has the world's biggest punk-rock band been up to? "We've just been jamming, screwing around," reports Nirvana bassist Krist Novoselic. "Kurt's got his family; we've all got our own trips. We just take things a lot slower now, instead of just being committed to the band. We do our thing."

Right now, the band is doing its thing in Seattle, where Novoselic, guitarist and proud papa Kurt Cobain and drummer Dave Grohl are working on material for a new album. Having recorded demos in October with legendary Seattle producer Jack Endino, who produced Nirvana's first album, *Bleach,* the band plans to record the album in the spring with Steve Albini, whose résumé includes the Pixies, Superchunk and Helmet. The album is due out this fall.

In the meantime, fans can make do with *Incesticide,* a rarities collection due out on Geffen/DGC Records on Dec. 15. Nirvana's first label, Sub Pop, was to release a similar collection, but the project went to DGC because, according to Novoselic, "Sub Pop was going to call it *Cash Cow* — that's violating," adding the band got more artistic control and better distribution through DGC. Sub Pop's Jonathan Poneman replies that "Krist has it all wrong — the record was going to be called *Piggy Bank.*"

Incesticide includes the 1990 Sub Pop single "Sliver"/"Dive"; most of *Hormoaning,* the much-sought-after compilation of BBC sessions released in Japan and Australia (including the live staple "Aneurysm" and covers of the Vaselines' "Molly's Lips" and an obscure Devo B side, "Turnaround"); and two unreleased early demos, "Hairspray Queen" and "Aero Zeppelin." The cover features a painting by Cobain.

"'Hairspray Queen' is one of the first things we ever did," says Novoselic. "'Aero Zeppelin,'" he adds, "couldn't be named anything else; it's just heavy cock-rock riffs. It gives that song a sense of humor."

Novoselic says it's hard to say exactly how Nirvana's next studio album will sound, noting that key *Nevermind* tracks such as "Smells Like Teen Spirit" were written just two weeks before recording. One thing's for sure: "It's not going to be as glossy and candy as *Nevermind,*" says Novoselic. "It's going to be more raw."

Besides beating the bootleggers, the band hopes the raw nature of the tracks on *Incesticide* will both prepare fans for the upcoming studio album and give them a little history lesson. "We thought it would be something nice for the fans just to see where we're coming from," says Novoselic. "Some of the stuff's kind of wild. Maybe the next step we'll take, because the pendulum is swinging back in that direction, won't be that much of a shock."

Nirvana will also split a single with the Jesus Lizard on the indie label Touch and Go. "Oh, the Guilt" will be released on Jan. 29. Meanwhile, Kurt Cobain will supply guitar feedback for an upcoming William Burroughs spoken-word album; he'll also produce the major-label debut (on Atlantic Records) of the ultra-heavy Northwest riff rockers the Melvins, a key early influence on Nirvana.

Novoselic is working on some side projects of his own. He recently helped win repeal of Washington State's so-called erotic-music law — which would have penalized retailers for selling certain types of unlabeled music to minors — by organizing meetings, attending press conferences and even hauling a PA system in his van. Nirvana itself headlined a benefit concert on Sept. 11 for the Washington State Music Coalition, the organization that lobbied against the law.

The bassist, who has supported decriminalization of marijuana, has another project upcoming. "All I'm going to say is, I'm working with hemp canvas," he says, "100 percent hemp canvas."

--- MICHAEL AZERRAD

INCESTICIDE

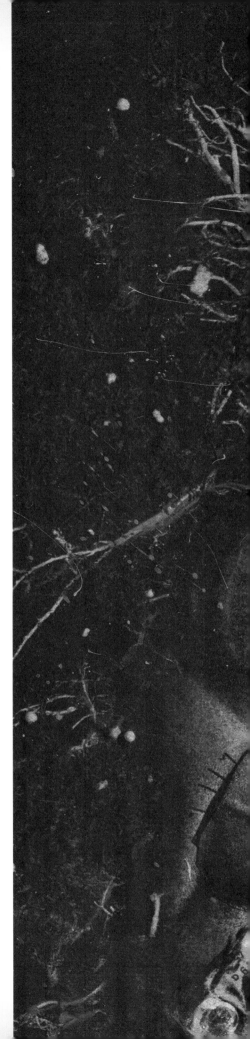

It is not easy to revisit one's published past, a process that yields greater sympathy for "Incesticide." Originally this appeared in "Rolling Stone" as a lead review combining "Incesticide" with Sub Pop's reissue of Blood Circus' recorded output, "Primal Rock Therapy." Both bands were there (wherever "there" was) at the beginning. The first time I saw Nirvana, they opened for Blood Circus (who in turn opened for the Leaving Trains), and back in 1988, Blood Circus seemed far more likely candidates for stardom.

Wrong on every count, as it turned out. Nirvana detested Blood Circus, which I discovered only after my review ran. Following its publication, I was somehow never granted another Nirvana interview. As for Blood Circus, they sold less than 100 CDs during the two weeks this issue of "Rolling Stone" was on the stands (I asked a friend at Sub Pop to keep track). And I am left with a final memory of Kurt, a pale, unshaven wraith in pajamas at a PJ Harvey show.

THE MEMBERS OF NIRVANA did not set out to become superstars, didn't expect to move millions of units, had no way to know that an entire generation was equally tired of being lied to — by their parents, by their government and by the music on the radio. They set out simply to write songs that spoke to their experience of the world and that felt good when played. Loud.

That insistence on emotional honesty is really all that connects the so-called Seattle bands; otherwise, Nirvana and Pearl Jam have nothing in common. Weird Al Yankovic lampooned Kurt Cobain's withdrawal into incoherence (remember the Who stuttering "My Generation"?), but laughing at "Smells Like Teen Spirit" misses the point: Some emotions are so deeply rooted that only the hideous abuse of an electric guitar and an untutored scream will do to express them. The Nirvana compilation, *Incesticide*, freezes fragments of a creative process that three or four years later miraculously caught the world's fancy. Back in 1989, when "Mexican Seafood" was recorded for C/Z's first *Teriyaki Asthma* compilation (it is remixed here), Nirvana was just three scrag-

gly guys from Aberdeen with bad equipment, half-formed ideas and a blue-collar aesthetic. *Incesticide* offers a glimpse at the process whereby they hammered melody to fury and came up with gold.

Incesticide was originally planned as a collection of otherwise unavailable remnants of Nirvana's early Sub Pop repertoire; its working title was said to be *Cash Cow*. The project moved to DGC, presumably to allow for a more comprehensive selection, but it's far from complete. Missing are splendid covers of the Velvet Underground, Kiss and the Wipers, plus a half-dozen live tracks released elsewhere and even some of *Nevermind*'s B sides. *Incesticide*'s tracks are scattered — in no particular order — and drawn from a variety of sources, including Nirvana's first 1987 demo ("Hairspray Queen"), the last Sub Pop single ("Sliver"/"Dive"), the Japanese-import EP *Hormoaning* (less two tracks), assorted BBC sessions and two local compilations.

The chaos of the collection suggests a struggle to diffuse the burdens of fame. Following *Nevermind* is a creative straitjacket. *Incesticide* presents Nirvana in a host of settings, including a whimsical cover of a Devo B side ("Turn Around") and a pair of tunes from the Vaselines ("Molly's Lips," "Son of a Gun"), the Scottish band since mutated into Eugenius. It exposes ragged early sessions ("Downer," "Mexican Seafood"), reinvents "(New Wave) Polly," a troubling song about rape, and revives "Dive," "Sliver" and "Aneurysm." It creates breathing room.

And that's the point: Nirvana was a great band before *Nevermind* topped the charts. *Incesticide* is a reminder of that and — maybe more important — proof of Nirvana's ability, on occasion, to fail. The unpolished forces at work and sometimes in conflict within the band are plainly exposed, as is a broader and rougher range of sounds, styles and interests.

That done, the group can go about writing and recording new material. With luck, perhaps *Incesticide* will remind Nirvana's audience that freedom to fail is the only useful definition of artistic freedom.

--- GRANT ALDEN

[April 9th, 1993]

LOUD FAST RULES
Nirvana Plays the Cow Palace
By Ann Powers

Hindsight is like one of those original apples from the tree of knowledge: once you've tasted it, it stays in your gut and changes your vision forever. Approaching this review again, after Kurt's crash, I'm struck by all the observations that could be read as signs: the references to manic-depression and disconnection; the sense that the band felt its fame to be a chore; the agony that emanated from the stage even then, almost a year before the suicide. While L7, the Breeders and the Disposable Heroes all seemed pleased (if bemused) at the chance to leave the particular edges where they'd grown up and face a bigger audience, Nirvana continued to represent the indie-rock scene's avant-garde belief in the bankruptcy of the mainstream. Yet the angry energy that allowed them to find power in this contradiction when they first broke had somehow dissipated, and what had once made the band's music feel revolutionary – its refusal to play by the old rules of Rock Star Monopoly – now appeared to drag it down.

These are the sentiments I expressed then, and hindsight advises I stick by them. But I can't simply back my opinion of Kurt Cobain's artistry into that corner and leave it there. The fact is, between the night of this concert and the afternoon I learned of Kurt's suicide, my skepticism about the hostility expressed throughout "Incesticide" – about the resolute failure to connect that hostility seemed to signal – had faded. I'd begun to see something much more complex in Nirvana's newer work. Kurt's repulsion at the rock-star ego trip was easy to taste, but beneath it he attempted to work a more complicated alchemy: to discover, using rock's language, an expression of power free of the usual machismo, authoritarianism and oppression of the feminine; to find the comfort in being sad, the strength in sometimes being weak, the messages in incoherence. His attempts to avoid the norm led Kurt toward a disappointingly common tragedy. But in his music, we can still find some new energy incubating, a hint of what kind of yes might have come after the no.

SAN FRANCISCO

IN THE '60s, rock and radicalism shared a utopian vision of transcendent unity. These days, however, our differences seem impossible to overcome, and rock's activists exhibit an odd, new cynicism. Discussing this benefit concert for Balkan rape victims, Nirvana's bassist, Krist Novoselic (the event's main organizer), stated that he didn't care if everyone in the audience understood the reason for the event. "We'll be getting their money anyway," he said. This attitude – screw the masses, do what you want – is essential to postpunk notions of integrity, and it drove Nirvana's frustrating performance.

Classic-rock epiphany isn't Nirvana's point; its music is powerful because it captures the state of manic-depression that seems to afflict our society en masse. The set started at top speed, with guitarist Kurt Cobain wailing, "Rape me!" and Novoselic and drummer Dave Grohl matching his outpouring of pain. Later, the audience sang along with the whimsical ode to disconnection "Lithium." Yet even such ironic moments of shared sensitivity were rare. "Smells Like Teen Spirit" seemed like a chore, and the band's new songs resembled alternative cuts on *Incesticide* rather than the hits on *Nevermind*.

Lyrics floated to the top of the murky mix like jetsam: "Suicide" rhymed with "I'm on your side"; phrases such as "All I know is all I know," "Everyone is gay" and "Go away" were screamed into exhaustion. Melodies emerged and sank again. The Cow Palace's lousy acoustics and the band's fascination with generating endless loops of fuzzy noise sabotaged the songs' occasional attempts at reaching beyond the insularity of a massive jam session. In a small club this refusal to stay within rock's conventions might have been revelatory, but in this arena it failed to translate.

The other bands on the bill were more successful at touching rock's old music without compromising their nontraditional ideals. Each band had new material and, unlike Nirvana, seemed thrilled at the chance to share it. The Breeders produced a bigger sound than they've previously managed, and guitarist Kim Deal reveled in her sassy star power.

Alternative rappers Disposable Heroes of Hiphoprisy filled the stage with carnivalesque special effects and dancing. Rappers Michael Franti and Rono Tse slipped once too often into hard-core hokum (I don't care if I never hear an audience shout, "Yo!" in unison again), but their rants against racism and violence radiated excitement.

Best of all was L7, Los Angeles' finest version of Kiss since the Runaways. Like both of those progenitors, this all-woman heavy-metal power unit lays on plenty of humor with its crunch. The band's newer songs seemed rawer than anything from its first album, but unlike the evening's headliners, L7 made these debuts into a party. The men in drag who serve as the group's go-go dancers, the mix of snot and snarl that shows up in the band members' vocals and their cartoonish rock-goddess stances onstage infused L7's set with that other quality that's always lifted rock's great performances above the swamp of the ordinary: good, dirty fun. ◐

IN UTERO

THIS IS THE WAY Nirvana's Kurt Cobain spells *success:* s-u-c-k-s-e-g-g-s. Never in the history of rock & roll overnight sensations has an artist, with the possible exception of John Lennon, been so emotionally overwhelmed by his sudden good fortune, despised it with such devilish vigor and exorcised his discontent on record with such bristling, bull's-eye candor.

In Utero is rife with gibes — some hilariously droll, others viciously direct — at life in the post-*Nevermind* fast lane, at the money-changers who milked the grunge tit dry in record time and at the bandwagon sheep in the mosh pit who never caught on to the desperate irony of "Here we are now, entertain us." The very first words out of Cobain's mouth in "Serve the Servants," *In Utero*'s petulant, bludgeoning opener, are "Teenage angst has served me well/Now I'm bored and old," sung in an irritated, marble-mouthed snarl that immediately derails any lingering expectations for a son of "Smells Like Teen Spirit."

It gets better. In "Very Ape," a two-minute corker cut from the same atomic-fuzz cloth as the band's 1989 debut album, *Bleach*, Cobain gets right down to brass tacks, against a burning-rubber lead-guitar squeal and the mantric rumble of bassist Krist Novoselic and drummer Dave Grohl: "I am buried up to my neck in/Contradictionary lies." (Nice pun, that.) The kiss-off quickly follows: "If you ever need anything, don't hesitate/To ask someone else first."

Cobain slightly overplays his hand with the title of "Radio Friendly Unit Shifter." Nirvana have been called many things over the past two years; that, as far as I can tell, is not one of them. But Cobain cuts right to the heart of the mire with a torrent of death-throe guitar feedback and a brilliant metaphor for the head-turning speed with which one man can suddenly sire a nation: "This had nothing to do with what you think/If you ever think at all. . . . / All of a sudden my water broke."

Frankly, Nirvana as a band and Cobain as the point man have earned the right to spit in fortune's eye. Generation X is really a generation hexed, caught in a spin cycle of updated '70s punk and heavy-metal aesthetics and cursed by the velocity with which even the most abrasive pop underculture can be co-opted and compromised. One minute, *Nevermind* is jackbooting Michael Jackson out of the No. 1 slot; the next, grunge jock Dan Cortese is screaming, "I love this place!" on behalf of Burger King. Even the hippies got a summer or two to themselves in the mid-'60s before the dough-re-mi boys horned in. So it's hardly a stretch to suggest that in "Frances Farmer Will Have Her Revenge on Seattle" (a slash-and-burner named after the locally born actress, whose rebellious streak brought her to the brink of insanity), it is really Cobain who wants to torch the town and send the A&R hounds packing.

None of this unrepentantly self-obsessed rant & roll would be half as compelling or convincing if Nirvana weren't such master blasters — Novoselic and Grohl deserve a few extra bows here — and Cobain wasn't a songwriter of such ferocious honesty and focused musical smarts. Cobain essentially works according to one playbook, but it's a winner no matter how he runs it. His songs invariably open with a slow-boil verse, usually sung in a plaintive groan over muted strumming and a tempered backbeat. Then Cobain vaporizes you with a chorus of immense power-chord static and primal howling. That, in a nutshell, is "Teen Spirit" and "Come As You Are." It also covers, to varying degrees, "Rape Me," "Pennyroyal Tea" and "Milk It" on *In Utero*.

But the devilry is in the details. "Rape Me" opens as a disquieting whisper, Cobain intoning the title verse in a battered croon, which sets you up beautifully to get blindsided by the explosive hook line.

In the sepulchral folk intro of "Pennyroyal Tea," Cobain almost sounds like Michael Stipe at the beginning of R.E.M.'s "Drive" – before the heaving, fuzz-burnt chorus comes lashing down with a vengeance.

Steve Albini's production, an au naturel power-trio snort that is almost monophonic in its compressed intensity, is particularly effective during those dramatic cave-ins. The word *grunge,* of course, doesn't do this kind of ravishing clatter justice. But Nirvana never bought into the simple Black Flag-cum-Sabbath hoodlum shtick anyway. From *Bleach* on, they have specialized in a kind of luminous roar and scarred beauty that has more to do with Patti Smith, the Buzzcocks and *Plastic Ono*-era John Lennon.

Actually, the icy tension of the part-ballad, part-punk-rock blues "Heart-Shaped Box" and the amorous chamber-punk urgency of "Dumb" ("My heart is broke/But I have some glue/Help me inhale/And mend it with you") confirm that if Generation Hex is ever going to have its own Lennon — someone who genuinely believes in rock & roll salvation but doesn't confuse mere catharsis with true deliverance — Cobain is damn near it. In "Heart-Shaped Box," the kind of song Stone Temple Pilots couldn't write even with detailed instructions, Cobain sets up a hypnotic coiled-spring tension between the frayed elegance of the verse melody and the strong Oedipal undertow of his obsession ("Throw down your umbilical noose so I can climb right back").

The last track, "All Apologies," is another stunning trump card, the fluid twining of cello and guitar hinting at a little fireside R.E.M. while the full-blaze pop glow of the chorus shows the debt of inspiration Cobain has always owed to Paul Westerberg and the vintage Replacements.

It's the last thing most people would expect from Angst Central, and it's an inspired sign-off that shows how Nirvana have been reborn in the face of suck-cess. *In Utero* is a lot of things — brilliant, corrosive, enraged and thoughtful, most of them all at once. But more than anything, it's a triumph of the will.

--- DAVID FRICKE

the on Road to

Nirvana

By Kim Neely

I suppose that everyone who ever met Kurt Cobain has some favorite memory of the singer – one enduring image that stands out. Mine is of Cobain leaning wearily on the counter at a taco joint in Davenport, Iowa, around midnight on Oct. 22, 1993.

I was never actually introduced to Cobain, and the 10 minutes or so I spent in his presence were more or less an accident. "Rolling Stone" had sent me out to cover the initial shows of Nirvana's first U.S. tour in two years. I'd hoped to talk with the band for the story and had been granted a much-coveted "All Access" pass, but it became apparent after I arrived in Kansas City and spoke with Nirvana's publicist, Jim Merlis, that the pass would be worthless if I tried to put it to use to corner the band members. Cobain, I was led to understand, was skittish about the press, and it would be a major problem if he learned that a "Rolling Stone" reporter was present. My status as persona non grata was reiterated an hour before show time, when Merlis, who'd earlier offered me a ride to the concert, called and informed me that I'd been booted. He'd been asked to drive Nirvana to the gig, he explained – would I mind taking a taxi? After the show, when Merlis headed backstage to say goodnight to the band, I made as if to follow him, and he politely let me know that it wasn't a good idea.

All this paranoia rubbed off. By the end of the Davenport show on the following night, I could imagine all manner of awful things happening if Cobain so much as caught a glimpse of me. I was so cowed that when Merlis and I were leaving the venue and Cobain and Dave Grohl stopped Merlis to ask him for a ride to the hotel, I actually ducked behind a speaker cabinet.

As we walked out to the car, a group of fans stopped Cobain and Grohl. I tried to get Merlis' attention and pull him aside – I was wondering whether I could hope to ask Cobain and Grohl a few questions on the way back to the hotel – but Merlis always seemed to be within earshot of Cobain; I couldn't get him alone.

Grohl and I got into the back of the car, and Cobain sat in the front passenger seat. I was in agony – acutely aware that this would be the only opportunity I had to talk to Cobain and Grohl, and just as aware that it would be a major faux pas if I whipped out my tape recorder and started firing off questions. Neither of them knew who I was or why I was there, and it was a horribly awkward situation.

A few minutes later, Cobain mentioned that he was hungry and asked Merlis to stop at a taco restaurant. There were a number of Nirvana fans inside the place, and as we waited for our order, Grohl went over to talk to them. Cobain signed an autograph for the one fan who mustered the courage to approach him, and then turned back to the counter.

The singer was wearing his ever-present mohair sweater. His clothes all but swallowed him, and as he waited there quietly, he seemed extremely weary and very frail. I remember thinking how incongruous it was that someone who seemed so passive and retiring could inspire so many people to walk on tacks around him.

Had I spent more time with Cobain, perhaps I would have come away with a different impression of him. But more than anything else as I watched him that night in Iowa, he struck me as someone adrift. There was an air of childlike compliance about him, as if he simply allowed himself to be swept along in whatever direction the current might take him. Since his death, I've been unable to shake that image of him, and I imagine I'll always think of Cobain the way he appeared to me on that night – as a lost Pisces who somehow, tragically, got caught in the undertow.

TWO CONVERSE HIGH TOPS, mismatched. One black Reebok. One tan loafer. One Birkenstock. The shoes, friends, never lie. And Nirvana's Oct. 22 blitz at Davenport, Iowa's Palmer Auditorium – judging from the array of ownerless footwear dotting the floor of the hall after the house lights went up – was at least a five-shoe affair on the rock & roll Richter scale.

In a town like Davenport, which usually doesn't make the cut when it comes to one-off shows, tickets for Nirvana's first U.S. tour in two years were probably the most coveted ducats of the year, a chance not only to see the band but to see it up close. Rejecting the arenas they could surely fill at this point, Nirvana are playing mostly 3,000 to 5,000-capacity general-admission venues. (The only exception to date: the opening show in Phoenix, where fans who paid the $6 admission to the Arizona State Fair could see Nirvana in the same 15,000-seat coliseum that Billy Ray Cyrus played the night before.)

Some pundits predicted that fans of Nirvana's last album, *Nevermind*, would be alienated by *In Utero*, given its rawer sound and Kurt Cobain's extremely personal outpourings of anguish and I-hate-fame bitterness. But if the Davenport audience was any indication, the majority are in it for the long haul. Scott McBride, a 22-year-old student from Cedar Falls who drove two and a half hours to see the Davenport gig, says he prefers the band's newest release to *Nevermind*.

"It's more straightforward," says McBride. "It makes more sense than *Nevermind*. I think he's putting his heart on the line, talking about what it's like for him to be what he is. I can't necessarily relate to it, but I understand him somewhat."

David Kemp, a 19-year-old student and musician who had never seen the band live before, gave Nirvana's performance an enthusiastic thumbs up. "It was bizarre," Kemp says of the crush on the floor. "I lasted five songs, and then I had to get out of there."

Some of the shows have fared better than others. The Oct. 18 Phoenix date drew rave reviews, while the following night's show, in Albuquerque, N.M., was reportedly spotty. In general, the Kansas City, Kan., show on Oct. 21 lacked energy, owing largely to Memorial Hall's poor acoustics, an absence of ventilation that turned the venue into a smoke-filled steam bath by the time Nirvana took the stage and a surprisingly jaded crowd that might as well have been standing, arms crossed, beneath a banner bearing the words HERE WE ARE NOW, ENTERTAIN US.

Cobain began the evening by wandering onto the stage while the house lights were still on. "Is Kevin here?" the singer asked. "My friend that I met last night? If you're here, raise your hand."

Hundreds of wise-asses promptly raised their hands, eliciting an exasperated shrug and a good-natured "Don't fuck with me" from Cobain. Kevin, it was revealed later, was a local drag queen the band had met the previous night; Cobain had his heart set on working him into the encore. But Kevin never showed, and the encore the Kansas City fans got instead – "Scentless Apprentice" and "On a Plain," followed by an almost unbearable 10 minutes of uninspired, feedback-laden wanking off – left the audience, aside from a few die-hard body surfers, looking restless and glassy eyed. Even Cobain seemed bored with the crowd's dogged insistence on hanging in there for every last ear-splitting shriek. "I'm not gonna turn my guitar off until you just go home," he warned the fans.

"You can stick around and listen to this bullshit if you want to." All told, aside from sterling versions of "About a Girl," "Come As You Are" and "Pennyroyal Tea" in the first third of the set, the show was a letdown.

Not so in Davenport. You wouldn't exactly expect the young inhabitants of this town – a sparsely populated farming community where nearly everything is named after tractor kingpin John Deere and the local entertainment listings boast such events as Riverbend Storytelling Guild Ghost Story Session and Great Pumpkin Day Sale – to outdo their more urban Kansas City peers in the kick-out-the-jams department, but they did. The youth of Davenport descended upon Palmer Auditorium like a plague of rowdy, yahooing locusts, and Nirvana, soaking up the crowd's rampant energy, turned in one of their most dazzling shows in recent memory. Within a few bars of the set-opening "Radio Friendly Unit Shifter," the floor of the hall was a writhing, cathartic jumble of bodies – a massive slam pit stretching clear to the exit doors and threatening to engulf the band's soundboard, which was protected by only one rickety barricade and three distinctly panicky-looking security guards.

From there, Nirvana – energetically abetted by former Germs guitarist Pat Smear and cellist Lori Goldston, who sat in on some of the acoustic numbers – took the ball and ran with it. Flanked by winged anatomical mannequins like the one featured on *In Utero*'s artwork, the band members bounced around a stage decorated like an enchanted forest – complete with creepy, dead-looking trees – and steamrollered in rapid-fire succession through "Drain You," "Breed," "Serve the Servants," "About a Girl," "Heart-Shaped Box,"

"Sliver," "Dumb," "In Bloom" and "Come As You Are." By the time they played "Lithium," they'd turned the audience into virtual puppets, a synchronized army that sang every word of the song's low-key verses and erupted into pogoing pandemonium every time the chorus rolled around. The band maintained the fever pitch with "Pennyroyal Tea" and "School," finally slowing the pace and giving the audience a breather with "Polly" and "Rape Me." The crowd response to the latter – 4,500 angelic voices softly crooning, "Rape me, my friend" – provided the evening's most surreal moment. It's doubtful that the parents of those present would understand why a song like "Rape Me" would attain anthem status. But their kids, the latchkey children of the Nasty '90s struggling to overcome the havoc wreaked on their psyches and their planet by the generation that preceded them, know why all too well.

Capping the hour with breakneck run-throughs of "Territorial Pissings" and "Smells Like Teen Spirit" (which Krist Novoselic introduced as "a song for our infomercial"), Nirvana left the stage, prompting what was easily the most thunderous demand for an encore heard by this reporter in five years. After returning for "Scentless Apprentice" and "Blew," Novoselic and Cobain hung their still-squealing guitars on the angel-like mannequins, leaving the dummies to bear not-so-silent witness to the fans as they filed out. Most of the departing concertgoers looked exhausted. But they also looked like they'd just witnessed the show of their lives, and it's doubtful that any of them – not even the five luckless mosh-pit casualties who shuffled into the 45-degree Iowa night one shoe poorer – had any complaints. ●

'I thought he was one of the more beautiful, quiet people. I always sensed this really intense sense of fantasy around him, through his music and a really intense sense of atmosphere." --CURT KIRKWOOD *singer, Meat Puppets*

Kurt Cobain:
The Rolling Stone
By David Fricke

[January 27th, 1994]

62

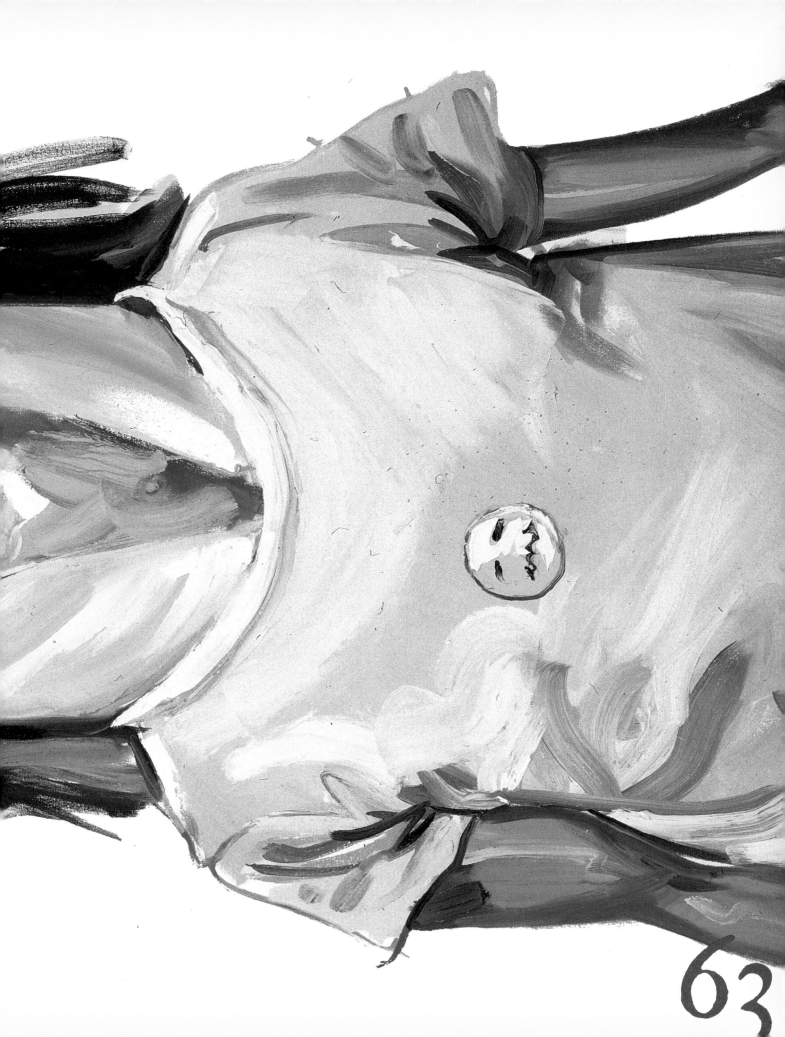

63

HIRTLESS, DISHEVELED KURT COBAIN pauses on the backstage stairway leading to Nirvana's dressing room at the Aragon Ballroom, in Chicago, offers a visitor a sip of his après-gig tea and says in a drop-deadpan voice, "I'm really glad you could make it for the shittiest show on the tour."

He's right. Tonight's concert — Nirvana's second of two nights at the Aragon, only a week into the band's first U.S. tour in two years — is a real stinker. The venue's cavernous sound turns even corrosive torpedoes like "Breed" and "Territorial Pissings" into riff pudding, and Cobain is bedeviled all night by guitar- and vocal-monitor problems. There are moments of prickly brilliance: Cobain's sandpaper howl cutting through the Aragon's canyonlike echo in the tense, explosive chorus of "Heart-Shaped Box"; a short, stunning "Sliver" with torrid power strumming by guest touring guitarist Pat Smear (ex-Germs). But there is no "Smells Like Teen Spirit," and when the house lights go up, so does a loud chorus of boos.

According to the Cobain press myth — "pissy, complaining, freaked-out schizophrenic," as he quite accurately puts it — the 26-year-old singer and guitarist should have fired the soundman, canceled this interview and gone back to his hotel room to sulk. Instead, he spends his wind-down time backstage, doting on his daughter, 1-year-old Frances Bean Cobain, a petite blond beauty who barrels around the room with a smile for everyone in her path. Later, back at the hotel, armed with nothing stronger than a pack of cigarettes and two minibar bottles of Evian water, Cobain is in a thoughtful, discursive mood, taking great pains to explain that success doesn't really suck — not as much as it used to, anyway — and that his life is pretty good. And getting better.

"It was so fast and explosive," he says in a sleepy, gravelly voice of his first crisis of confidence following the ballistic success of *Nevermind.* "I didn't know how to deal with it. If there was a Rock Star 101 course, I would have liked to take it. It might have helped me.

"I still see stuff, descriptions of rock stars in some magazine — 'Sting, the environmental mental guy,' and 'Kurt Cobain, the whiny, complaining, neurotic, bitchy guy who hates everything, hates rock stardom, hates his life.' And I've never been happier in my life. Especially within the last week, because the shows have been going so well — except for tonight. I'm a much happier guy than a lot of people think I am."

Cobain took some long, hard detours to get there over the past year. The making of *In Utero,* Nirvana's long-awaited studio follow-up to *Nevermind,* was fraught with last-minute title and track changes as well as a public scrap between the band, its record label, DGC, and producer Steve Albini over the album's commercial potential — or lack thereof. Cobain's marriage to punk-noir singer Courtney Love of the band Hole — dream fodder for rock gossips since the couple exchanged vows in February 1992 — made headlines again last June when Cobain was arrested by Seattle police for allegedly assaulting Love during a domestic fracas. Police found three guns in the house, but no charges were filed, and the case was dismissed.

Last year, Cobain also made a clean breast of his long-rumored heroin addiction, claiming he'd used the drug — at least in part — to opiate severe, chronic stomach pain. Or as he puts it in this interview, "to medicate myself." He's now off the junk, and thanks to new medication and a better diet, his digestive tract, he says, is on the road to recovery.

But the roots of his angst, public and personal, go much deeper. Born near the logging town of Aberdeen, Wash., Cobain is — like Nirvana's bassist, Krist Novoselic, drummer Dave Grohl and a high percentage of the band's young fans — the product of a broken home, the son of an auto mechanic and a secretary who divorced when he was 8. Cobain had early aspirations as a commercial artist and won a number of high-school art contests; he now designs much of Nirvana's artwork. (He made the plastic-fetus collage on the back cover of *In Utero,* which got the record banned by Kmart and Wal-Mart.) But after graduation, Cobain passed on an art-school scholarship and took up the teen-age-bum life, working as a roadie for the local punk band the Melvins (when he was working at all) and applying himself to songwriting.

"I never wanted to sing," Cobain insists now. "I just wanted to play rhythm guitar — hide in the back and just play. But during those high-school years when I was playing guitar in my bedroom, I at least had the intuition that I had to write my own songs."

For a long time, after Nirvana catapulted from junior Sub Pop-label signees to grunge supergods — they won the Best Band and Best Album trophies in ROLLING STONE's 1994 Critics' Poll — Cobain could not decide whether his talent was a blessing or a curse. He has finally come to realize it's a bit of both. He is bugged that people think of him more as an icon than a songwriter yet fears that *In Utero* marks the finish line of the Nirvana sound crystallized in "Smells Like Teen Spirit." Cobain remains deeply mistrustful of the music business but says he has done a complete U-turn on his attitude toward Nirvana's mass punk-wanna-be flock.

"I don't have as many judgments about them as I used to," Cobain says, almost apologetically. "I've come to terms about why they're there and why we're here. It doesn't bother me anymore to see this Neanderthal with a mustache, out of his mind, drunk, singing along to 'Sliver.' That blows my mind now.

"I've been relieved of so much pressure in the last year and a half," Cobain says with discernible relief in his voice. "I'm still kind of mesmerized by it." He ticks off the reasons for his content: "Pulling this record off. My family. My child. Meeting William Burroughs and doing a record with him.

"Just little things that no one would recognize or care about," he continues. "And it has a lot to do with this band. If it wasn't for this band, those things never would have happened. I'm really thankful, and every month I come to more optimistic conclusions."

"I just hope," Cobain adds, grinning, "I don't become so blissful I become boring. I think I'll always be neurotic enough to do something weird."

A long with everything else that went wrong onstage tonight, you left without playing "Smells Like Teen Spirit." Why?

That would have been the icing on the cake [*smiles grimly*]. That would have made everything twice as worse.

I don't even remember the guitar solo on "Teen Spirit." It would take me five minutes to sit in the catering room and learn the solo. But I'm not interested in that kind of stuff. I don't know if that's so lazy that I don't care anymore or what. I still like playing "Teen Spirit," but it's almost an embarrassment to play it.

In what way? Does the enormity of its success still bug you?

Yeah. Everyone has focused on that song so much. The reason it gets a big reaction is, people have seen it on MTV a million times. It's been pounded into their brains. But I think there are so many other songs that I've written that are as good, if not better, than that song, like "Drain You." That's definitely as good as "Teen Spirit." I love the lyrics, and I never get tired of playing it. Maybe if it was as big as "Teen Spirit," I wouldn't like it as much.

But I can barely, especially on a bad night like tonight, get through "Teen Spirit." I literally want to throw my guitar down and walk away. I can't pretend to have a good time playing it.

But you must have had a good time writing it.

We'd been practicing for about three months. We were waiting to sign to DGC, and Dave [Grohl] and I were living in Olympia [Wash.], and Krist [Novoselic] was living in Tacoma [Wash.]. We were driving up to Tacoma every night for practice, trying to write songs. I was trying to write the ultimate pop song. I was basically trying to rip off the Pixies. I have to admit it [*smiles*]. When I heard the Pixies for the first time, I connected with that band so heavily I should have been in that band — or at least in a Pixies cover band. We used their sense of dynamics, being soft and quiet and then loud and hard.

"Teen Spirit" was such a clichéd riff. It was so close to a Boston riff or "Louie, Louie." When I came up with the guitar part, Krist looked at me and said, "That is so ridiculous." I made the band play it for an hour and a half.

Where did the line "Here we are now, entertain us" come from?

That came from something I used to say every time I used to walk into a party to break the ice. A lot of times, when you're standing around with people in a room, it's really boring and uncomfortable. So it was "Well, here we are, entertain us. You invited us here."

How did it feel to watch something you'd written in fun, in homage to one of your favorite bands, become the grunge national anthem, not to mention a defining moment in youth marketing?

Actually, we did have our own thing for a while. For a few years in Seattle, it was the Summer of Love, and it was so great. To be able to just jump out on top of the crowd with my guitar and be held up and pushed to the back of the room and then brought back with no harm done to me — it was a celebration of something that no one could put their finger on.

But once it got into the mainstream, it was over. I'm just tired of being embarrassed by it. I'm beyond that.

This is the first U.S. tour you've done since the fall of '91, just before "Nevermind" exploded. Why did you stay off the road for so long?

I needed time to collect my thoughts and readjust. It hit me so hard, and I was under the impression that I didn't really need to go on tour, because I was making a whole bunch of money. Millions of dollars. Eight million to 10 million records sold — that sounded like a lot of money to me. So I thought I would sit back and enjoy it.

I don't want to use this as an excuse, and it's come up so many times, but my stomach ailment has been one of the biggest

barriers that stopped us from touring. I was dealing with it for a long time. But after a person experiences chronic pain for five years, by the time that fifth year ends, you're literally insane. I couldn't cope with anything. I was as schizophrenic as a wet cat that's been beaten.

How much of that physical pain do you think you channeled into your songwriting?

That's a scary question, because obviously if a person is having some kind of turmoil in their lives, it's usually reflected in the music, and sometimes it's pretty beneficial. I think it probably helped. But I would give up everything to have good health. I wanted to do this interview after we'd been on tour for a while, and so far, this has been the most enjoyable tour I've ever had. Honestly.

It has nothing to do with the larger venues or people kissing our asses more. It's just that my stomach isn't bothering me anymore. I'm eating. I ate a huge pizza last night. It was so nice to be able to do that. And it just raises my spirits. But then again, I was always afraid that if I lost the stomach problem, I wouldn't be as creative. Who knows? [*Pauses*] I don't have any new songs right now.

Every album we've done so far, we've always had one to three songs left over from the sessions. And they usually have been pretty good ones that we really liked, so we always had something to rely on — a hit or something that was above average. So this next record is going to be really interesting, because I have absolutely nothing left. I'm starting from scratch for the first time. I don't know what we're going to do.

One of the songs that you cut from "In Utero" at the last minute was "I Hate Myself and I Want to Die." How literally did you mean it?

As literal as a joke can be. Nothing more than a joke. And that had a bit to do with why we decided to take it off. We knew people wouldn't get it; they'd take it too seriously. It was totally satirical, making fun of ourselves. I'm thought of as this pissy, complaining, freaked-out schizophrenic who wants to kill himself all the time. "He isn't satisfied with anything." And I thought it was a funny title. I wanted it to be the title of the album for a long time. But I knew the majority of the people wouldn't understand it.

Have you ever been that consumed with distress or pain or rage that you actually wanted to kill yourself?

For five years during the time I had my stomach problem, yeah. I wanted to kill myself every day. I came very close many times. I'm sorry to be so blunt about it. It was to the point where I was on tour, lying on the floor, vomiting air because I couldn't hold down water. And then I had to play a show in 20 minutes. I would sing and cough up blood.

This is no way to live a life. I love to play music, but something was not right. So I decided to medicate myself.

Even as satire, though, a song like that can hit a nerve. There are plenty of kids out there who, for whatever reasons, really do feel suicidal.

That pretty much defines our band. It's both those contradictions. It's satirical, and it's serious at the same time.

What kind of mail do you get from your fans these days?

[*Long pause*] I used to read the mail a lot, and I used to be really involved with it. But I've been so busy with this record, the video,

the tour, that I haven't even bothered to look at a single letter, and I feel really bad about it. I haven't even been able to come up with enough energy to put out our fanzine, which was one of the things we were going to do to combat all the bad press, just to be able to show a more realistic side of the band.

But it's really hard. I have to admit I've found myself doing the same things that a lot of other rock stars do or are forced to do. Which is not being able to respond to mail, not being able to keep up on current music, and I'm pretty much locked away a lot. The outside world is pretty foreign to me.

I feel very, very lucky to be able to go out to a club. Just the other night, we had a night off in Kansas City, Mo., and Pat [Smear] and I had no idea where we were or where to go. So we called up the local college radio station and asked them what was going on. And they didn't know! So we happened to call this bar, and the Treepeople from Seattle were playing.

And it turns out I met three really, really nice people there, totally cool kids that were in bands. I really had a good time with them, all night. I invited them back to the hotel. They stayed there. I ordered room service for them. I probably went overboard, trying to be accommodating. But it was really great to know that I can still do that, that I can still find friends.

And I didn't think that would be possible. A few years ago, we were in Detroit, playing at this club, and about 10 people showed up. And next door, there was this bar, and Axl Rose came in with 10 or 15 bodyguards. It was this huge extravaganza; all these people were fawning over him. If he'd just walked in by himself, it would have been no big deal. But he *wanted* that. You create attention to attract attention.

Where do you stand on Pearl Jam now? There were rumors that you and Eddie Vedder were supposed to be on that "Time" magazine cover together.

I don't want to get into that. One of the things I've learned is that slagging off people just doesn't do me any good. It's too bad, because the whole problem with the feud between Pearl Jam and Nirvana had been going on for so long and has come so close to being fixed.

It's never been entirely clear what this feud with Vedder was about.

There never was one. I slagged them off because I didn't like their band. I hadn't met Eddie at the time. It was my fault; I should have been slagging off the record company instead of them. They were marketed — not probably against their will — but without them realizing they were being pushed into the grunge bandwagon.

Don't you feel any empathy with them? They've been under the same intense follow-up-album pressure as you have.

Yeah, I do. Except I'm pretty sure that they didn't go out of their way to challenge their audience as much as we did with this record. They're a safe rock band. They're a pleasant rock band that everyone likes. [*Laughs*] God, I've had much better quotes in my head about this.

It just kind of pisses me off to know that we work really hard to make an entire album's worth of songs that are as good as we can make them. I'm gonna stroke my ego by saying that we're better than a lot of bands out there. What I've realized is that you only need a couple of catchy songs on an album, and the rest can be

bullshit Bad Company rip-offs, and it doesn't matter. If I was smart, I would have saved most of the songs off *Nevermind* and spread them out over a 15-year period. But I can't do that. All the albums I ever liked were albums that delivered a great song, one after another: Aerosmith's *Rocks*, the Sex Pistols' *Never Mind the Bollocks . . .*, *Led Zeppelin II*, *Back in Black*, by AC/DC.

You've also gone on record as being a big Beatles fan.

Oh, yeah. John Lennon was definitely my favorite Beatle, hands down. I don't know who wrote what parts of what Beatles songs, but Paul McCartney embarrasses me. Lennon was obviously disturbed [*laughs*]. So I could relate to that.

And from the books I've read — and I'm so skeptical of anything I read, especially in rock books — I just felt really sorry for him. To be locked up in that apartment. Although he was totally in love with Yoko and his child, his life was a prison. He was imprisoned. It's not fair. That's the crux of the problem that I've had with becoming a celebrity — the way people deal with celebrities. It needs to be changed; it really does.

No matter how hard you try, it only comes out like you're bitching about it. I can understand how a person can feel that way and almost become obsessed with it. But it's so hard to convince people to mellow out. Just take it easy, have a little bit of respect. We all shit [*laughs*].

"In Utero" may be the most anticipated, talked-about and argued-over album of 1993. Didn't you feel at any point during all the title changes and the press hoopla stirred up by Steve Albini that the whole thing was just getting stupid? After all, it is just an album.

Yeah. But I'm used to it [*laughs*]. While making the record, that wasn't happening. It was made really fast. All the basic tracks were done within a week. And I did 80 percent of the vocals in one day, in about seven hours. I just happened to be on a roll. It was a good day for me, and I just kept going.

So what was the problem?

It wasn't the songs. It was the production. It took a very, very long time for us to realize what the problem was. We couldn't figure it out. We had no idea why we didn't feel the same energy that we did from *Nevermind*. We finally came to the conclusion that the vocals weren't loud enough, and the bass was totally inaudible. We couldn't hear any notes that Krist was playing at all.

I think there are a few songs on *In Utero* that could have been cleaned up a little bit more. Definitely "Pennyroyal Tea." That was not recorded right. There is something wrong with that. That should have been recorded like *Nevermind*, because I know that's a strong song, a hit single. We're toying with the idea of re-recording it or remixing it.

You hit and miss. It's a really weird thing about this record. I've never been more confused in my life, but at the same time I've never been more satisfied with what we've done.

Let's talk about your songwriting. Your best songs — "Teen Spirit," "Come As You Are," "Rape Me," "Pennyroyal Tea" — all open with the verse in a low, moody style. Then the chorus comes in at full volume and nails you. So which comes first, the verse or the killer chorus?

[*Long pause, then he smiles*] I don't know. I really don't know. I guess I start with the verse and then go into the chorus. But I'm getting so tired of that formula. And it is formula. And there's not

much you can do with it. We've mastered that — for our band. We're all growing pretty tired of it.

It is a dynamic style. But I'm only using two of the dynamics. There are a lot more I could be using. Krist, Dave and I have been working on this formula — this thing of going from quiet to loud — for so long that it's literally becoming boring for us. It's like "OK, I have this riff. I'll play it quiet, without a distortion box, while I'm singing the verse. And now let's turn on the distortion box and hit the drums harder."

I want to learn to go in between those things, go back and forth, almost become psychedelic in a way but with a lot more structure. It's a really hard thing to do, and I don't know if we're capable of it — as musicians.

Songs like "Dumb" and "All Apologies" do suggest that you're looking for a way to get to people without resorting to the big-bang guitar effect.

Absolutely. I wish we could have written a few more songs like those on all the other albums. Even to put "About a Girl" on *Bleach* was a risk. I was heavily into pop, I really liked R.E.M., and I was into all kinds of old '60s stuff. But there was a lot of pressure within that social scene, the underground — like the kind of thing you get in high school. And to put a jangly R.E.M. type of pop song on a grunge record, in that scene, was risky.

We have failed in showing the lighter, more dynamic side of our band. The big guitar sound is what the kids want to hear. We like playing that stuff, but I don't know how much longer I can scream at the top of my lungs every night, for an entire year on tour. Sometimes I wish I had taken the Bob Dylan route and sang songs where my voice would not go out on me every night, so I could have a career if I wanted.

So what does this mean for the future of Nirvana?

It's impossible for me to look into the future and say I'm going to be able to play Nirvana songs in 10 years. There's no way. I don't want to have to resort to doing the Eric Clapton thing. Not to put him down whatsoever; I have immense respect for him. But I don't want to have to change the songs to fit my age [*laughs*].

The song on "In Utero" that has whipped up the most controversy is "Rape Me." It's got a brilliant hook, but there have been objections to the title and lyric — not just from skittish DJs but from some women who feel it's rather cavalier for a man to be using such a potent, inflammatory word so freely.

I understand that point of view, and I've heard it a lot. I've gone back and forth between regretting it and trying to defend myself. Basically, I was trying to write a song that supported women and dealt with the issue of rape. Over the last few years, people have had such a hard time understanding what our message is, what we're trying to convey, that I just decided to be as bold as possible. How hard should I stamp this point? How big should I make the letters?

It's not a pretty image. But a woman who is being raped, who is infuriated with the situation . . . it's like "Go ahead, rape me, just go for it, because you're gonna get it." I'm a firm believer in karma, and that motherfucker is going to get what he deserves, eventually. That man will be caught, he'll go to jail, and *he'll* be raped. "So rape me, do it, get it over with. Because you're gonna get it worse."

What did your wife, Courtney, think of the song when she heard it?

I think she understood. I probably explained it better to her than I've explained it to you. I also want to make a point, that I was really, honestly not trying to be controversial with it. That was the last thing I wanted to do. We didn't want to put it out so it would piss off the parents and get some feminists on our asses, stuff like that. I just have so much contempt for someone who would do something like that [to a woman]. This is my way of saying: "Do it once, and you may get away with it. Do it a hundred times. But you're gonna get it in the end."

When you were arrested on the domestic-violence charge this summer, Courtney admitted to the police that you kept guns in your home. Why do you feel you need to be armed?

I like guns. I just enjoy shooting them.

Where? At what?

[*Laughs*] When we go out to the woods, at a shooting range. It's not an official shooting range, but it's allowed to be one in this county. There's a really big cliff, so there's no chance of shooting over the cliff and hurting anyone. And there's no one within miles around.

Without getting too PC about it, don't you feel it's dangerous to keep them in the house, especially with your daughter, Frances, around?

No. It's protection. I don't have bodyguards. There are people way less famous than I am or Courtney who have been stalked and murdered. It could be someone by chance looking for a house to break into. We have a security system. I actually have one gun that is loaded, but I keep it safe, in a cabinet high up on a shelf where Frances can never get to it.

And I have an M-16, which is fun to shoot. It's the only sport I have ever liked. It's not something I'm obsessed with or even condone. I don't really think much of it.

How does Courtney feel about keeping guns at home?

She was there when I bought them. Look, I'm not a very physical person. I wouldn't be able to stop an intruder who had a gun or a knife. But I'm not going to stand by and watch my family stabbed to death or raped in front of me. I wouldn't think twice of blowing someone's head off if they did that. It's for protection reasons. And sometimes it's fun to go out and shoot. [*Pauses*] At targets. I want to make that clear [*laughs*].

People usually assume that someone who has sold a few million records is really livin' large. How rich are you? How rich do you feel? According to one story, you wanted to buy a new house and put a home studio in it, but your accountant said you couldn't afford it.

Yeah, I can't. I just got a check a while ago for some royalties for *Nevermind*, which is pretty good size. It's weird, though, really weird. When we were selling a lot of records during *Nevermind*, I thought, "God, I'm gonna have like $10 million, $15 million." That's not the case. We do not live large. I still eat Kraft macaroni and cheese — because I like it, I'm used to it. We're not extravagant people.

I don't blame any kid for thinking that a person who sells 10 million records is a millionaire and set for the rest of his life. But it's not the case. I spent a million dollars last year, and I have no idea how I did it. Really. I bought a house for $400,000. Taxes were another $300,000-something. What else? I lent my mom some money. I bought a car. That was about it.

You don't have much to show for that million.

It's surprising. One of the biggest reasons we didn't go on tour when *Nevermind* was really big in the States was because I thought: "Fuck this, why should I go on tour? I have this chronic stomach pain, I may die on this tour, I'm selling a lot of records, I can live the rest of my life off a million dollars." But there's no point in even trying to explain that to a 15-year-old kid. I never would have believed it.

Do you worry about the impact that your work, lifestyle and ongoing war with supercelebrity are having on Frances? She seemed perfectly content to toddle around in the dressing room tonight, but it's got to be a strange world for her.

I'm pretty concerned about it. She seems to be attracted to almost anyone. She loves anyone. And it saddens me to know that she's moved around so much. We do have two nannies, one full-time and another older woman who takes care of her on weekends. But when we take her on the road, she's around people all the time, and she doesn't get to go to the park very often. We try as hard as we can, we take her to preschool things. But this is a totally different world.

In "Serve the Servants," you sing, "I tried hard to have a father/But instead I had a dad." Are you concerned about making the same mistakes as a father that might have been made when you were growing up?

No. I'm not worried about that at all. My father and I are completely different people. I know that I'm capable of showing a lot more affection than my dad was. Even if Courtney and I were to get divorced, I would never allow us to be in a situation where there are bad vibes between us in front of her. That kind of stuff can screw up a kid, but the reason those things happen is because the parents are not very bright.

I don't think Courtney and I are that fucked up. We have lacked love all our lives, and we need it so much that if there's any goal that we have, it's to give Frances as much love as we can, as much support as we can. That's the one thing that I know is not going to turn out bad.

What has been the state of relations within Nirvana over the past year?

When I was doing drugs, it was pretty bad. There was no communication. Krist and Dave, they didn't understand the drug problem. They'd never been around drugs. They thought of heroin in the same way that I thought of heroin before I started doing it. It was just really *sad*. We didn't speak very often. They were thinking the worst, like most people would, and I don't blame them for that. But nothing is ever as bad as it seems. Since I've been clean, it's gone back to pretty much normal.

Except for Dave. I'm still kind of concerned about him, because he still feels like he can be replaced at any time. He still feels like he . . .

Hasn't passed the audition?

Yeah. I don't understand it. I try to give him as many compliments as I can. I'm not a person who gives compliments very often, especially at practice. "Let's do this song, let's do that song, let's do it over." That's it. I guess Dave is a person who needs reassurance sometimes. I notice that, so I try and do that more often.

So you call all the shots?

Yeah. I ask their opinions about things. But ultimately, it's my decision. I always feel weird saying that; it feels egotistical. But we've *never* argued. Dave, Krist and I have never screamed at each other. Ever.

It's not like they're afraid to bring up anything. I always ask their opinion, and we talk about it. And eventually, we all come to the same conclusions.

Haven't there been any issues where there was at least heated discussion?

Yeah, the songwriting royalties. I get all the lyrics. The music, I get 75 percent, and they get the rest. I think that's fair. But at the time, I was on drugs when that came up. And so they thought that I might start asking for more things. They were afraid that I was going to go out of my mind and start putting them on salary, stuff like that. But even then we didn't yell at each other. And we split everything else evenly.

With all of your reservations about playing "Smells Like Teen Spirit" and writing the same kind of song over and over, do you envision a time when there is no Nirvana? That you'll try to make it alone?

I don't think I could ever do a solo thing, the Kurt Cobain Project.

Doesn't have a very good ring to it, either.

No [*laughs*]. But yes, I would like to work with people who are totally, completely the opposite of what I'm doing now. Something way out there, man.

That doesn't bode well for the future of Nirvana and the kind of music you make together.

That's what I've been kind of hinting at in this whole interview. That we're almost exhausted. We've gone to the point where things are becoming repetitious. There's not something you can move up toward, there's not something you can look forward to.

The best times that we ever had were right when *Nevermind* was coming out and we went on that American tour where we were playing clubs. They were totally sold out, and the record was breaking big, and there was this *massive* feeling in the air, this vibe of energy. Something really special was happening.

I hate to actually even say it, but I can't see this band lasting more than a couple more albums, unless we really work hard on experimenting. I mean, let's face it. When the same people are together doing the same job, they're limited. I'm really interested in studying different things, and I know Krist and Dave are as well. But I don't know if we are capable of doing it together. I don't want to put out another record that sounds like the last three records.

I know we're gonna put out one more record, at least, and I have a pretty good idea what it's going to sound like: pretty ethereal, acoustic, like R.E.M.'s last album. If I could write just a couple of songs as good as what they've written. . . . I don't know how that band does what they do. God, they're the greatest. They've dealt with their success like saints, and they keep delivering great music.

That's what I'd really like to see this band do. Because we are stuck in such a rut. We have been labeled. R.E.M. is what? College rock? That doesn't really stick. Grunge is as potent a term as New Wave. You can't get out of it. It's going to be passé. You have to take a chance and hope that either a totally different audience accepts you or the same audience grows with you.

And what if the kids just say, "We don't dig it, get lost"?

Oh, well. [*Laughs*] Fuck 'em. ◉

'Kurt could just be very outgoing and funny and charming, and a half hour later he would just go sit in the corner and be totally moody and uncommunicative. And I would ask Krist, 'Is he OK?' And Krist would say, 'He's all right --- sometimes he's just quiet. And then he'd be fine again.

--- BUTCH VIG producer, *Nevermind,*

Courtney *Speaks Her Mind*

[December 23rd, 1993]

BY KIM NEELY

I didn't know what to expect when I talked to Courtney Love for the first time. By early November 1993, when this interview took place, the singer's unapologetic bluntness and propriety-be-damned demeanor – not to mention her marriage to Kurt Cobain – had made her a favorite target of music-industry wags, and conventional wisdom held that Courtney was a woman to be reckoned with whether you wanted to reckon with her or not. Rumor had it that she liked to call people at all hours of the morning and rant at them endlessly, that she loved to gossip, that she was unabashed about letting fly with withering tirades about those she perceived as enemies. I'd been told that the foremost concern when interviewing Courtney was not to run out of tape. Before we actually talked, my image of her was of someone who would talk at you as opposed to with you; I suppose I expected a loud, abrasive harridan who would ramble on at hyperspeed and probably not make much sense.

At the time, Love had been out of the headlines for some months, focusing her attention on her daughter, Frances Bean, and on the recording of Hole's second album, "Live Through This." It took a good month of phone calls between Hole's management and "Rolling Stone" before Love agreed to be interviewed: The singer was still angry about the 1992 "Vanity Fair" article that had nearly caused her and Cobain to lose custody of Frances, and she was also reluctant to do a solo interview. Weary of the media's tendency to focus only on her, Love wanted Hole to be presented as a band. Eventually she consented to the interview.

When Love called on the appointed evening, I found that I liked her instantly. She was friendly, quick-witted and utterly without pretense; not once during our conversation did I get the impression that she was editing her opinions for print. I also found her to be unusually inquisitive. It's rare – and a little disconcerting – for an interview subject to turn the tables on you and begin asking questions, but Love did this so often that several times I felt as if I were the one being interviewed.

At the start of our conversation, Love told me somewhat apologetically that she wasn't "in a gossipy mood." Despite this, we talked for four hours, and she answered most of my questions before I got a chance to ask them. Because she was calling on a cellular phone from Nirvana's tour bus, there were occasional interruptions. At one point, the bus made a stop at a convenience store, and Love had me hold on while she asked Cobain to buy "Huggies, and some snacky things – Hostess stuff." Several times, as the bus drove in and out of the cellular's range, we were disconnected by loud bursts of static. Each time this happened, Love would call back and pick up the thread of the conversation. We finally wound down at around six in the morning, Love offering a sleepy, "I had a good time, good night," before she hung up. As I went to bed that morning, I remember thinking that there was a lot more to Courtney Love than most people seemed to give her credit for.

Because of space limitations in the issue of "Rolling Stone" in which this interview first appeared, a good deal of the conversation wound up on the cutting-room floor. The interview is presented here in its original, unexpurgated form for the first time.

COURTNEY LOVE isn't the type to shun notoriety, but for the past few years, the outspoken vocalist has been a household name for all the wrong reasons. Back in 1991, Love was simply known as a rising talent. But just as the momentum behind her band Hole was peaking, Love made what was, in hindsight, a fairly bad career move: She married Nirvana frontman Kurt Cobain. Almost instantly, gossip about Love's relationship with her superstar spouse overshadowed her career. The furor reached the boiling point in September 1992, when a now-infamous *Vanity Fair* article alleged that Love took heroin after she knew she was pregnant with her daughter, Frances Bean – an accusation Love denies vehemently – causing a firestorm of controversy.

This year seems to have been more to Love's liking. Frances Bean is now 15 months old and a rosy-cheeked charmer; motherhood clearly agrees with Love; and she and her band (guitarist Eric Erlandson, bassist Kristen Pfaff and drummer Patty Schemel) are putting the finishing touches on their major-label debut, aptly titled *Live Through This*.

Calling via cellular phone from the Nirvana tour bus, where she was visiting her husband just before the start of her own tour with the Lemonheads, Love was funny, impressively savvy and unfailingly direct.

How are you doing?

Well, I lost a piece of jewelry and I'm really freaking out about it. It was an actual diamond.

What happened?

I left it in a Fed-Ex package under the sofa in Kurt's dressing room. I think someone will find it. I think the caterers probably will find it, and they won't give it back 'cause they think I'm rich. It's really depressing. It wasn't my wedding ring, but it was practically my wedding ring. It was my anniversary ring to myself. Someone will find it and just think, "Oh, she's rich."

You never know. It depends who finds it.

Yeah. I've found like 10 wallets in my life, and I've always given them back. Always.

Well, do you want to get started?

Yeah, sure. You gotta ask me a lot of questions, 'cause I'm not really in a gossipy mood.

OK. What did 1993 represent for you?

Was *Vanity Fair* this year? No, that was last year. Um . . . this year was good! It was about being leveled by something and finding a higher ground. It was about trying to find ideal songs in myself with the kind of competition I'm up against in my own house, which is pretty intense. This year has been about growth. And I'm a mother, and it's great. I don't care if that's a cliché. It really *is* great.

How has that changed you?

You know what? That's such a personal question. There's some kind of mother blood that just makes you want to buy firearms when you have a child. She's like this perfection, this innocence, this utter and total purity that's uncorrupted by anything. And if somebody were to hurt or deride or in any way fuck with my child, I would not hesitate to kill them. I'll answer anything, but on every level that that question operates, it's just too personal. It's too deep.

OK. Let's talk about the new album. How is it most different from "Pretty on the Inside"?

Well, it's leaps and bounds different. It's so different that there should've been a record in between. I didn't want a punk-rock record – I did that. So it's very melodic, and there are a lot more harmonies. And you know, because our songwriting is so different, it's hard to deal with. We played in Atlanta on Halloween, and all these weird purists showed up. Total fans, but every time we'd go into one of our pop songs, they'd start chanting: "Don't do it! Sellout!" I heard one girl saying to this other girl, "They *used* to be so much better." So I just started talking to the audience. I said, "I've grown, you haven't, the sex really isn't good anymore, and you know what? There's always gonna be a shitty band with girls in it that can't play." Girls were throwing riot grrrl 'zines at me and stuff. I was like, "Uh, I'm really glad you're here, girls, but check it out: I can write a bridge now."

Fans don't tend to deal well with change.

When I was making *Pretty on the Inside*, I had just been kicked out of Babes in Toyland, and I had a real chip on my shoulder. I was like, "I'm gonna be the angriest girl in the world, fuck you!" I didn't want to have a crack in my surface and put anything *jangly* on there. I really wish that I had put something pretty on there. I mean, I'm glad people don't expect much from me, but at the same time, I wish that they had an inkling that I had an inkling of how to write.

Do you really think that's the case – that people don't expect much from you? You've gotten a lot of flack in the press, but I don't know that that's the case with fans . . .

See, when you say "the press" – this bugs me, because I can count on one hand the fallacious pieces that have been written about me. And basically you're talking about one piece in one magazine. I want to clarify that. It isn't "the press." It's never been "the press." It was one article. It's the result of one woman's interpretation of my character and my life, whatever her insane and fucked-up agenda might have been.

But there has been a tendency for the press to focus more on your marriage than your music, and there've been insinuations that you married Kurt to boost your career.

Well, that surprised me. There's nothing in my past to indicate that I've gone out with anything but loser guys. That's sort of my pattern, anyway. So it was a nice surprise that my husband turned out to be successful, but it wasn't something I expected or counted on. You know, you think you're getting into a liberal art, but you're basically getting into the NFL. It's as exclusively male as major-league sports. You still have to deal with the idea that women are taught to marry the doctor and be the nurse. Or be the head cheerleader and date the football captain. It's really sick. If you've ever been to, like, a *Rip* magazine party or something, and you're in the women's bathroom, it's *depressing* in there. You give those girls the ability to play, and the instrument of their choice, and they'll just be repulsed by the idea. They don't see any empowerment in that, or any kind of sexual validation. The only sexual validation they have is who they sleep with. And I wasn't raised to think like that. This is something I've always wanted to do. I had my first guitar when I was really young. When I saw that Runaways record, I was like, "This is it – this is what I'm gonna do." And I knew it was a novel idea in some ways, but I thought merit would prevail. I had a more liberal idea of how it would be, because of the way I was raised. My mother was a feminist, and I basically believed in Santa Claus. I was pretty stupid.

How else has sexism manifested itself in terms of your career?

I just heard last night that [Lollapalooza organizer] Mark Geiger said, "We really want Nirvana to play Lollapalooza – tell Kurt that Courtney can play if he plays." I was really disgusted by that. I called him today, and I was gonna give him the tongue-lashing of his life. Talk about underestimating someone's intelligence. "Uh, OK, Courtney, I'm gonna do Lollapalooza, so you can open." *Please.* First of all, I would never, ever, ever play with Kurt. No matter how good it felt or how right it was. Your intentions can be great, but the world's gonna interpret it differently. And even if Kurt wasn't doing it, I'd get it anyway. So it's a *disadvantage* for me for Kurt to do it, if I wanted to do it. That shocked me, that he thinks we're that stupid.

Are you fairly active, in a feminist sense?

I guess I am, on the one hand, but I'm not, on the other. I'm obviously an activist feminist, but I'm not an academic. I'm not a scholar, and I'm not involved heavily in any groups. Other than Susan Faludi's thing, which I really like.

"Backlash" was an amazing book.

Wasn't that great? I've purchased 30 or 40 copies of that book, and handed them out primarily to writers. But I have a lot of friends in bands that can't get through it because, "It makes me too *aaaaangrrrrry.*" You know. "I'm getting too *maaad.*"

Those are the same people who pay to see a movie and then cover their eyes during the gritty parts.

I kind of do that, too.

Do you really?

Well, like the part in *Platoon* when Willem Defoe gets killed by Tom Berenger. I had to turn the channel. And there's a scene in *The King of Comedy* — which I've seen like a hundred times — that I still can't watch.

Which scene?

It's when Rupert goes up to the office and starts making an ass of himself, and then he has to deal with Shelley Hack, and she's like [*adopts a condescending, businesslike purr*] "Mr. Pupkin . . . Mr. Pupkin . . ." I just can't stand that! Rupert Pupkin is in everybody. Everybody has a Rupert Pupkin inside of them. I certainly do. And it scares me. I know the dialogue to that entire movie. That and *Caligula.*

I must be the only person on the planet who never saw "Caligula."

I had to work at a topless bar in Guam. I went to Guam to pout because I didn't get the part of Nancy Spungen [in Alex Cox's film *Sid & Nancy*]. And thank God I didn't get Nancy Spungen. [*Laughs*] Can you *imagine?* Anyway, I ended up working in a topless bar, and they had three videos there: a Filipino porn movie, a Japanese porn movie and *Caligula.* I was there for three weeks, and every night, I'd put on *Caligula* twice. For my whole shift, that would be our movie. That's when I started getting obsessed with the whole Roman thing.

How so?

Well, it's like, who *were* these people? Why is it upheld as some sort of great civilization? In my opinion, the fact that it was so well documented is to our detriment. It was a male utopia. First of all, they had slaves in a big way. Second of all, their marriages were totally arranged, there were no marriages out of love. People like to compare it to the decadence today, but the decadence was far more rampant than it is here now. And you know, you could make yourself a god in the senate. It would be like going to Congress and saying, "OK, I'm a god. I'm replacing Jesus and all the Halloween decorations in school. Me. I'm a god." Which is the real reason Christianity was born. I think Christ was born right around the time that everyone was declaring themselves a god. What Christ did was not really new — it was just kind of the going thing at the time: "I'm the Messiah." But with him, it just caught on. I'm serious! There were tons of people who were saying they were messiahs at the time. It was a big deal to be a messiah. I'm just sort of obsessed with that time, because it's always held up as an example of degeneracy and also sophistication, and yet there were probably many more-sophisticated societies. What were we talking about before I got off on this tangent?

Feminism and Susan Faludi.

Yeah. I met her, and I hung out with her one day. I was scared shitless. Believe it or not, I couldn't even really talk. I talked about the history of women in music, and I'd made a little map for her. But she scared me. All that brain crammed into that little head! And she's really lovely. She has a lot of grace, a lot of poise, and she's actually really beautiful. Not in a poofy-haired Naomi Wolf kind of way.

Naomi Wolf gets on my nerves. She's not nearly as poetic or brilliant.

There's another book I read called *Words and Women.* It's a real slim volume, and it sounds boring and looks boring, but it's just as well written and clever as *Backlash.* Do you know that in the Merriam Webster dictionary, the word *manly* is described as a complimentary adjective, and the word *womanly* is described as an insult? They use sentences with the words in them, i.e., "She took it like a man," or "You're behaving in a very womanly manner, stop it." It's in there right now! That kind of thing is very subtle, but it's very important. Language really traps us.

You can find a lot of examples of that kind of thing if you really think about it.

I'm like the Spike Lee of women or something. "Everywhere I look, there's *prejudice!*" But you just see it. When I was reading *Words and Women,* I was noticing *everything.* Kurt's one of the most liberal people I know, but he looked at me one day, and he goes, "I hate it when you read those fucking feminist books." It was so funny. 'Cause it was like, you know, everything was a conspiracy.

It isn't even a deliberate thing, though. It's just this insidious ignorance in the way society views male and female roles. For example, if someone wants to insult a male rock critic, it's always, "Oh, he's just a frustrated musician." But nobody ever says that about female journalists. They say, "Oh, she just got into this to meet guys in bands."

Good point. That's a great point. Because I've never thought of a female writer as a frustrated musician. See, it's even in my own brain — I ghettoize, too!

I read somewhere that you had a gripe with female musicians who talk about wanting to "rock like the guys." Does that still hold?

Well, I guess that happens because there aren't a lot of female role models. I mean, I think Debbie Harry's a very nice person, and I think she had a really droll delivery and was cool, and I loved her attitude, but she's not one of my role models. Obviously, Madonna's not a role model of mine — Madonna or anybody who's that sexual. Women don't have people to look to who've already done it. It's an archetype that's undefined. Where you have the male archetype, that's so easy, you know? "Oh, he's the whining rock star." "Oh, he's the messiah rock star." "Oh, he's the coke-doing, model-dating rock star." So a lot of girls, I think, fall into a trap of "Well, if I want to be taken seriously, I've got to denounce my gender — act like a man, dress like a man, do it as good as the guys and completely lose touch with my femininity." It's really hard for them to find their identity when they're in a band, because they don't have an archetype to either rebel against or look up to. Except for Chrissie Hynde, who's always been backed by men. And you need role models, you really do. Otherwise you're in the dark. So in a lot of ways, it's really exciting. For us, it's the beginning of our rock history. I mean, it goes all the way back to the beginning of rock & roll, from the Gingerbreads to all the Phil Spector-era singing bands to the late '60s and early '70s, bands like Isis and Fanny and Bertha. They all kind of blew. But I think they thought, "Wow, this is really free and cool, we can play music now." And they still couldn't break that barrier. The barrier's just now breaking.

To a certain extent, anyway.

Yeah. When *Nevermind* came out, I was in Chicago with Kat [Bjelland, Babes in Toyland vocalist], and we were in a bar. We got

so drunk we got thrown out of the bar — we were so mad. They were playing *Nevermind* on the stereo, and we just kept looking at each other, and I just knew what she was thinking, and vice versa. It was like, "It's great that this happened, but if you or I had written this record, it would've sold a hundred thousand." We both knew that. We didn't even need to say anything to each other. We just knew it. We had chosen to take this challenge and start our band and fucking do something, and yet there's this goddamn glass ceiling.

How competitive are you musically, and who do you see as your primary competition?

Well, that's a great word, isn't it? Is there only room for one of us? Is that why people would like to reduce it to some sort of mud wrestling?

I'm not talking just female competition. I mean competition in general.

I think I'm competitive in an American, good way. I don't think I'm competitive in a shitty way. I'm not a bad sport; I want to respect my enemy. You know, when we toured with Mudhoney, I would walk in their dressing room every night: "Jerks, punks, are you ready? 'Cause I'm gonna kick your ass." I've always been that way, and it inspires me. It's what makes me go. Not insurmountable odds, but interesting, fun stuff. Like, "God, if she can do it or he can do it, I can do it too!" All of the Pixies' records were amazing to me, so I felt very competitive in terms of the way that Kim Deal and Charles [Thompson] wrote songs. And the way that Kurt wrote songs. Back when Kurt was just, like, a guy that I thought was a bit of a dick, I heard "In Bloom" in my publicist's office, and it really woke me up. I find his songwriting to be impeccable. Lyric-wise — and this sounds very insane and pretentious — if I could just turn a phrase as well as Leonard Cohen, I'd be pleased. I mean, he's like what, 55, and he can still pull that shit off? The guy's fucking amazing. Throughout any trends I've gone through, I've always had one of my Leonard tapes. I like Joni Mitchell's *Blue* a lot. It's kind of sad and weird.

Who else inspired you?

I was totally white trash. *Rumours* was a big influence on me. Everyone's like: "Liz Phair, that's a parody of *Exile on Main Street*. And I'm like, "Yeah, well, this record is a parody of *Rumours*."

I think Stevie Nicks is due for a comeback.

Well, she's a major influence on me. I love her. She's like the spangly, sparkly Gold Dust fucking Woman.

Who else?

Mostly, I have Echo and the Bunnymen and Psychedelic Furs roots. People don't admit that 'cause it's so uncool. I'm like, "That's my roots, man." I never said I was punk. If you watch *Suburbia*, that was the West Coast punk scene. Sexist, lame poseurs, everybody trying to be the Rolling Stones. It was ugly. That's the thing I hated about it: It was so ugly, and everything smelled. I wanted some glamour. Some celebrity fabulousness! Do you have New Wave roots?

No, not really. But I was the first kid on my block to have "Never Mind the Bollocks." I had it on 8-track.

[*To Cobain*] She bought the Sex Pistols on 8-track! That's hardcore!

Do you still have it? Kurt says he'll give you $150 for it.

It's long gone. Probably in a landfill somewhere.

Did you like the Stooges and stuff?

Yeah. But the first band I was ever seriously into was the Beatles.

Oh, yeah, me too. Which record?

The first one I had was one of those greatest-hits collections. There was a red one and a blue one. I had the blue one.

Which is 1967-1970. That's the one that has "Hey Jude" on it. I love that song. I totally get in arguments with people about Paul. I could do it for hours, the merits of Paul. Like if there was no Paul, there would be no "Helter Skelter." If there had been no "Helter Skelter," there would be no Sonic Youth. That's true. [*Cobain is heard protesting in the background.*] This is a really good ancient argument of ours. Kurt always goes: "Oh? Who played the chords?" I don't care. Paul wrote the song. No one sticks up for Paul. Actually, there's a real Paul song on our record, called "Miss World."

What kind of stuff did you write about on this record? The past few years have been uphill for you. Did any of that seep into the new lyrics?

This record is not as obvious, and it's not as personal. You know, when women say, "Well, I play music, and it's cathartic," that applies to me to a degree, but it's also really not fair to ghettoize people like that. Whether it's Joni Mitchell or PJ Harvey or me, it's like you're supposed to be looking through a keyhole at a nervous breakdown. That's what you're supposed to be seeing. And I just think that's fucking lame. If I write a song with an old Stooges riff about being a teenage prostitute, that doesn't mean that I was a teenage prostitute, any more than it means that Neil Young shot his girlfriend at the river or Kurt raped Polly. You know what I'm saying? These are narratives. I just wanted to write a good rock record. I would love to write a couple of great rock songs in my life, like Chrissie Hynde did. She's really the only person of my gender who I find completely accomplished, because as much as I love Patti Smith, she didn't write her own music. Because when you write a great song, there's nothing more important or better. I mean, not *anything*. Not any kind of shitty values about beauty, fame, shallowness, money, drugs or any of that crap. If you write something that will transcend a long period of time and make people feel a certain way, there's really nothing like that.

It seems really important to you to leave a mark.

Yeah. To me, that's what's important in terms of my work. I mean, what was the Walt Whitman quote about when you die, leaving a fertile patch of grass and a happy child? When you're dying and your life is flashing before your eyes, I don't think you're gonna be thinking about how much you hate some journalist. You're gonna be thinking about the great things that you did, the horrible things that you did, the emotional impact that someone had on you and that you had on somebody else. Those are the things that are relevant. To have some sort of emotional impact that transcends your time, that's great. As long as you don't mess it up by being undignified when you're old.

What do you think you'll be like when you're old?

I hope that I'll be dignified. I *know* I won't be pathetically addicted to any kind of bullshit. I'd like to have a really large brood of children and a good garden, and I'd like to grow really great hybrid roses and have a lot of dogs and a lot of cats and get *Victoria* magazine and have a goddamn nice house! I don't think I want to be sitting on a porch drinking whiskey and singing the blues. [*Laughs*] Knowing me, I'd probably end up at a bar, asking some guy to get me another martini. Still bleaching my hair at 59. ◐

"It's the sort of thing where you hear it and you just keep thinking about it but you can never quite make yourself believe that it's totally true. You hear it and see it on the news -- like 24 hours on MTV or something like that --- but at the same time it doesn't really sink in that you're never going to see this person onstage again. Or there's never going to be another Nirvana record. That's the sort of day to-day, real-life thing that hasn't really sunk in."

--- MAC

MACCAUGHAN
lead singer, Superchunk

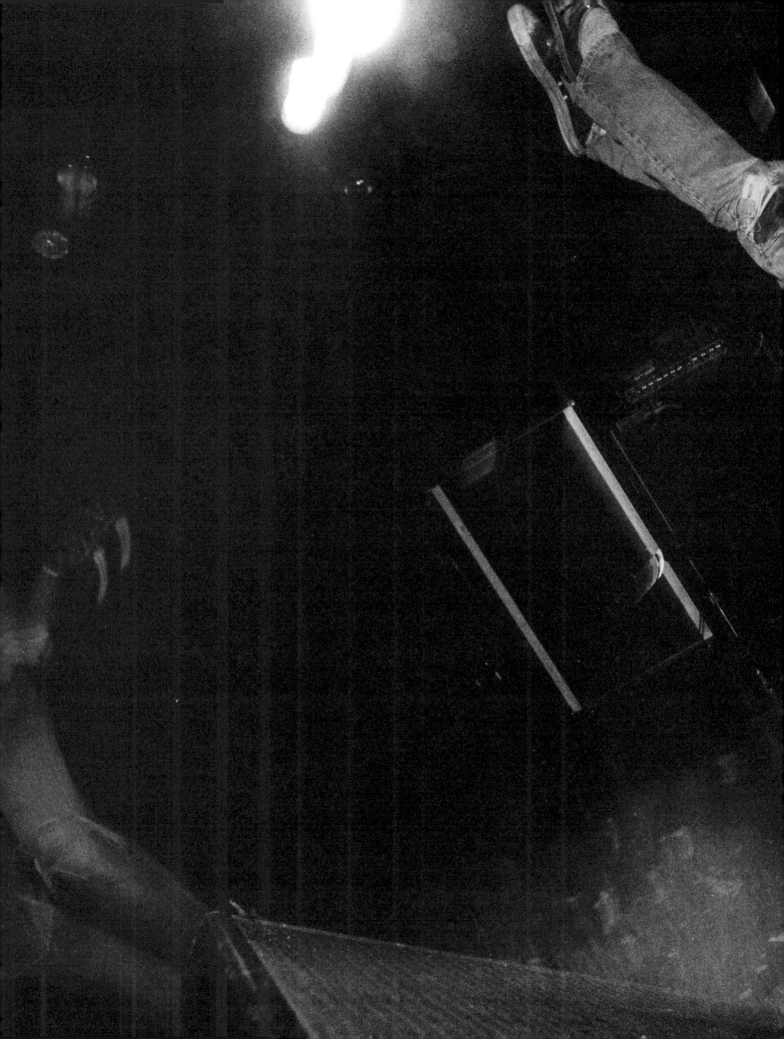

N APRIL 8, shortly before 9 a.m., Kurt Cobain's body was found in a room above the garage of his Seattle home. Across his chest lay the 20-gauge shotgun with which the 27-year-old singer, guitarist and songwriter ended his life. Cobain had been missing for six days.

Gary Smith, an electrician installing a security system in the house, discovered Cobain dead. "At first I thought it was a mannequin," Smith said afterward. "Then I noticed it had blood in the right ear. Then I saw a shotgun lying across the chest, pointing up at his chin."

Though the police, a private-investigation firm and friends were on the trail, his body had been lying there for two and a half days, according to a medical-examiner's report. A high concentration of heroin and traces of Valium were found in Cobain's bloodstream. He was identifiable only by his fingerprints.

Mark Lanegan, a member of Screaming Trees and a close friend of Cobain's, says he didn't hear from Cobain that last week. "Kurt hadn't called me," he says. "He hadn't called some other people. He hadn't called his family. He hadn't called anybody." Lanegan says he had been "looking for [Kurt] for about a week . . . before he was found. . . . I had a feeling that something real bad had happened."

Cobain's friends, family and associates had been worried about his depression and chronic drug use for years. "I was involved in trying to get Kurt professional help on numerous occasions," says former Nirvana manager Danny Goldberg, now president of Atlantic Records. It wasn't, however, until eight days after Cobain returned to Seattle from Rome to recuperate from a failed suicide attempt in March that those close to him realized that it was time to resort to drastic measures. Cobain had gone "cuckoo," says a spokesperson for Gold Mountain Entertainment, the company that manages Nirvana and Hole.

Those who were friends with Cobain and his wife, Courtney Love, report an increase in domestic disputes during that period, including instances when Love was forced to spend nights away from the house in order to escape Cobain's erratic behavior. Cobain had even told a few friends that he was worried Love was having an affair.

His relationship with Nirvana was just as rocky. In fact, Love told MTV that Cobain said to her in the weeks after Rome: "I hate it. I can't play with them anymore." She added that he only wanted to work with Michael Stipe of R.E.M.

"In the last few weeks, I was talking to Kurt a lot," Stipe said in a statement. "We had a musical project in the works, but nothing was recorded."

On March 18, a domestic dispute escalated into a near disaster. After police officers, summoned by Love, arrived at the scene, she told them that her husband had locked himself in a room with a .38-caliber revolver and said he was going to kill himself. The officers confiscated that gun as well as a bottle of "assorted," unidentified pills that the singer had on him. Love told the officers where Cobain had stashed a Beretta .380 handgun, a Taurus .38 handgun, a Colt semiautomatic rifle and 25 boxes of ammunition, all of which was confiscated. Though, later that night, Cobain told officers that he hadn't actually been planning to take his own life, the police report nonetheless described the incident as a "volatile situa-

tion with the threat of suicide." No one was arrested, and Cobain "left the residence" afterward.

Four days later, Cobain and Love took a taxi from their home in Seattle's Madrona neighborhood to the American Dream used-car lot near downtown Seattle. The taxi driver, Leon Hasson, says the couple fought the whole ride there. Still arguing, Cobain and Love entered the lot. According to lot owner Joe Kenney, Love was upset because a few days after they had purchased a Lexus on Jan. 2, Cobain had returned it. Love wanted the car, but Cobain wanted something less ostentatious. Kenney adds that Love appeared unstable and dropped several pills while walking toward a bathroom.

By this time, Cobain's family members, band mates and management company had begun talking to a number of intervention counselors about treating Cobain's increasing heroin and psychological problems. One of these specialists was Steven Chatoff, executive director of Anacapa by the Sea, a behavioral health center for the treatment of addictions and psychological disorders, in Port Hueneme, Calif. "They called me to see what could be done," says Chatoff. "He was using, up in Seattle. He was in full denial. It was very chaotic. And they were in fear for his life. It was a crisis."

Chatoff began interviewing friends, family members and business associates in preparation for enacting a full-scale intervention. According to Chatoff, someone then tipped off Cobain, and the procedure had to be canceled. Gold Mountain claims that it found another intervention counselor and told Chatoff a small lie to turn down his services politely.

Meanwhile, Roddy Bottum, an old friend of Love and Cobain's and the keyboardist for Faith No More, flew from San Francisco to Seattle to care for Cobain. "I really loved Kurt," Bottum says, "and we got along really well. I was there to be with him as a friend."

The Downward

Nirvana bassist Krist Novoselic staged his own separate intervention with Cobain, but the most grueling confrontation took place on March 25. That afternoon, roughly 10 friends — including band mates Novoselic and Pat Smear, Nirvana manager John Silva, longtime friend Dylan Carlson, Love, Goldberg and Hole's manager Janet Billig — gathered at Cobain's home on Seattle's Lake Washington Boulevard to take a different approach with a new intervention counselor. As part of the intervention, Love threatened to leave Cobain, and Smear and Novoselic said they would break up the band if Cobain didn't check into rehab. At first, Cobain was unwilling to admit he had a drug problem and did not believe that his recent behavior had been self-destructive. By the end of the tense five-hour session, however, Cobain's resolve had weakened, and he agreed to enter a detox program in Los Angeles later that day. He then retired to the basement with Smear, where they rehearsed some new material.

Once at the Seattle airport, though, Cobain changed his mind and refused to board the flight. Love had hoped to coax Cobain into flying to Los Angeles with her so that the couple could check into rehab together. Instead, she wound up on a plane with Billig. (The couple's daughter, Frances Bean, and a nanny followed the next day.) Love would say that she regretted leaving Cobain alone ("That '80s tough-love bullshit, it doesn't work," she said in a taped message during a memorial vigil for Cobain two weeks later). After a stop in San Francisco, Billig and Love flew to Los Angeles, and on the morning of March 26, Love checked into a $500-a-night suite in the Peninsula Hotel in Beverly Hills, and began an outpatient program to detox from drugs (Gold Mountain says it was tranquilizers).

Back in Seattle that evening, Cobain stopped by a woman friend and drug dealer's house in the upscale, bohemian Capitol Hill district. "Where are my friends when I need them?" she told a Seattle newspaper Cobain said to her. "Why are my friends against me?"

Cobain stayed in Seattle five more days before agreeing to go to Los Angeles for treatment. Before leaving, he stopped by Carlson's condominium in the Lake City area of Seattle to ask for a gun because Carlson, who was the best man at Cobain and Love's wedding, says Cobain told him there were trespassers on his Madrona property. "He seemed normal — we'd been talking," Carlson says. "Plus, I'd loaned him guns before." Though there is no registration or waiting period for shotguns in Seattle, Carlson believes Cobain didn't want to buy the shotgun himself because he was afraid the police would confiscate it, since they had taken his other firearms after the domestic dispute that had occurred 12 days earlier.

Cobain and Carlson headed to Stan's Gun Shop nearby and purchased a six-pound Remington Model 11 20-gauge shotgun and a box of ammunition for roughly $300, which Cobain gave Carlson in cash. "He was going out to L.A.," Carlson says. "It

On April 1, Cobain called Love, who was still at the Peninsula. "He said, 'Courtney, no matter what happens, I want you to know that you made a really good record,' " she later told a Seattle newspaper. "I said, 'Well, what do you mean?' And he said, 'Just remember, no matter what, I love you.'" (Hole were due to release their second album, *Live Through This*, 11 days later.) That was the last time Love spoke to her husband.

According to an artist known as Joe Mama, a longtime friend of the couple's who was the last to visit Cobain at Exodus: "I was ready to see him look like shit and depressed. He looked so fucking great." An hour later, Cobain, in Love's words, "jumped the fence." Actually, it was a six-foot-plus brick wall surrounding the center's patio.

Though Exodus is a low-security clinic, and Cobain could have walked out the door if he had wanted to, he had something else in mind. One of Cobain's visitors recalls: "When I went to visit him, Gibby Haynes [of the Butthole Surfers] was in there with him. I don't know Gibby, but he's a nut. He was jabbering a mile a minute about people who had jumped over the wall there, stuff like '[one guy] went over the wall five times.' Kurt probably thought it would be funny."

At 7:25 p.m., Cobain told the clinic staff he was stepping out onto the patio for a smoke and scaled the wall. "We watch our patients really well," says a spokesperson for Exodus. "But some do get out." Most of Cobain's friends and business associates then in L.A. were at a concert by another Gold Mountain client, the Breeders, oblivious to the fact that he had escaped.

"After Kurt left, I was on the phone with Courtney all the time," says Mama. "She was really freaked out, so we drove around looking for him at all the places he might have gone. She was really scared from the beginning. I guess she could tell."

S P I R A L *By Neil Strauss*

seemed kind of weird that he was buying the shotgun before he was leaving. So I offered to hold onto it until he got back." Cobain, however, insisted on keeping the shotgun himself. The police believe that Cobain brought the weapon home and stashed it in a closet. Novoselic reportedly drove Cobain to the airport. Smear and a Gold Mountain employee met Cobain in Los Angeles and drove him to the Exodus Recovery Center, in the Daniel Freeman Marina Hospital, in Marina del Rey, Calif. Cobain had spent four days detoxing at Exodus in 1992 but left the center before his treatment was completed.

Despite his inability to proceed with his plan, Chatoff says he spoke with Cobain by phone several times before Cobain left for Los Angeles. "I was not supportive of that at all," says Chatoff of Cobain's admittance to Exodus, "because that was just another detox 'buff and shine.' "

Cobain spent two days at the 20-bed clinic. He talked to several psychologists there, none of whom considered him suicidal. Though Frances Bean and her nanny visited him, Love never did.

But Cobain was already on his way back to Seattle. He returned home on a Delta flight three hours after his escape, arriving in Seattle at 1 a.m. By the time Love canceled his Seafirst bank credit card and hired private investigator Tom Grant to track him down the following day, it was too late. In fact, according to police, canceling the credit card made it even more difficult to find Cobain because Seafirst only records the type of business and amount of money for attempted charges on canceled cards, not the precise location of the business. Love also reportedly hired a second private investigator to watch the home of Cobain's drug dealer, a woman of whom Love is said to have been jealous to begin with.

When Cobain returned to his Madrona home, he found his daughter's former nanny, Michael DeWitt (whose nickname is Cali), staying there. "I talked to Cali, who said he had seen [Kurt] on Saturday [April 2]," says Carlson, adding that DeWitt described Cobain as looking ill and acting weird, "but I couldn't get a hold of him myself."

Neither could anybody else. The police believe Cobain wan-

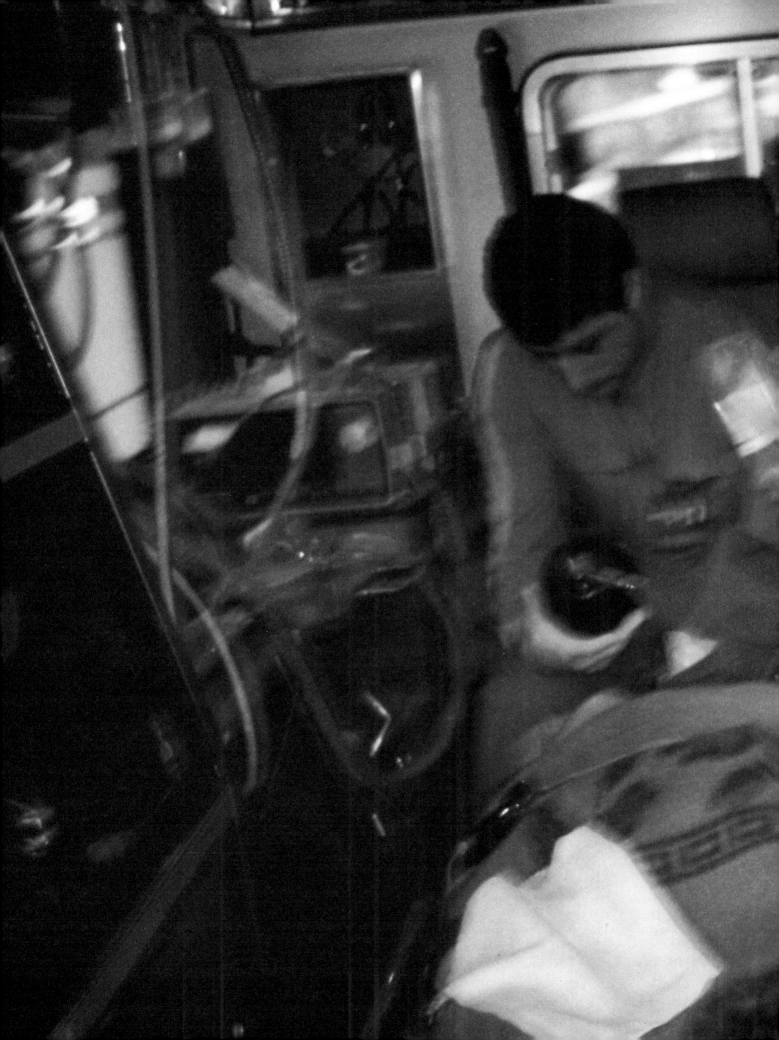

dered around town with no clear agenda in his final days. A taxi supervisor reports that Cobain was driven to a gun shop to buy shotgun shells (a receipt for the ammo was later found at Cobain's house). Neighbors say they spotted Cobain in a park near his house during this period, looking ill and wearing an incongruously thick jacket. Cobain reportedly spent time with some junkie friends, shooting up so much that they kicked him out because they were worried that he'd OD on them. Cobain is also believed to have spent time at his second home, in Carnation, Wash., where a sleeping bag was found. Next to it was a picture of the sun drawn in black ink above the words "cheer up," and an ashtray filled with cigarettes – one brand was Cobain's, the other wasn't.

On Sunday, April 3, someone (possibly Cobain) attempted to make several charges to his credit card. The amounts, ranging from $1,100 to $5,000, were apparent attempts to get cash. The following day, two more charge attempts were made, this time to get $86.60 worth of flowers. It was this same day that Cobain's mother, Wendy O'Connor, filed a missing-person's report. She told police that Cobain might be suicidal and suggested that they look for him at a particular three-story brick building, described as a location for narcotics, in Capitol Hill.

Sometime on or before the afternoon of April 5, Cobain barricaded himself in the room above his garage by propping a stool against its French doors. The evidence at the scene suggests that he removed his hunter's cap – which he wore when he didn't want people to recognize him – and dug into the cigar box that contained his drug stash. He completed a one-page note in red ink. Addressing the note to "Boddah," the name he had given his childhood imaginary friend, Cobain spoke of the great empty hole he felt had opened inside, turning him into a "miserable, self-destructive death rocker." He also expressed his terror that Frances Bean's life would turn out like his own. Calling Love "a goddess of a wife who sweats ambition and empathy," he implored her to "please keep going" for their child's sake.

"I haven't felt the excitement of listening to as well as creating music, along with really writing . . . for too many years now," Cobain scrawled, adding that "when we're backstage and the lights go out and the manic roar of the crowd begins, it doesn't affect me the way in which it did for Freddie Mercury. . . . I've tried everything within my power to appreciate it, and I do, God, believe me, I do. But it's not enough. I appreciate the fact that I and we have affected and entertained a lot of people. I must be one of those narcissists who only appreciate things when they're gone. I'm too sensitive. I need to be slightly numb in order to regain the enthusiasm I had as a child."

Cobain apparently tossed his wallet on the floor, which was open to his Washington driver's license; friends believe this was to help the police identify him. Love reconstructed the rest of the tragedy for MTV: Cobain drew a chair up to the window, sat down, took some more drugs (most likely heroin), pressed the barrel of the 20-gauge shotgun to his head and – evidently using his thumb – pulled the trigger.

Though the county medical examiner has determined that Cobain died on the afternoon of April 5, someone tried to charge a $1,517.56 cash advance on his credit card the following morning. The attempt was either made over the phone or in person without

the card. The police also report that two people say that Cobain's Capitol Hill heroin dealer told them Cobain had come by her apartment the night of April 5. The dealer denies the incident.

In a cruel twist of fate, it wasn't until April 6 that Love's private investigator, Tom Grant, arrived in Seattle. "I was working with [Grant]," Carlson says, "and the day we were going to Carnation to look for him, we found out he was dead."

Carlson and Grant, a former deputy sheriff, had checked Cobain's Madrona home twice but failed to search the apartment above the garage, where Cobain's body lay. (Carlson later stated that he had no knowledge of the existence of a room above the garage.) DeWitt left the main house and flew to Los Angeles on the afternoon of April 7, still unaware of the body nearby. Police say they never entered the house before Cobain's body was found, only asking workers outside his house if they had seen Cobain.

Elsewhere on April 7, an emergency phone call was placed to 911 about a "possible overdose victim" at the Peninsula Hotel in Los Angeles. The police, the fire department and ambulances arrived at the scene, where they found Love and Hole guitarist Eric Erlandson. (Frances Bean and her nanny were staying in the room next door.) Love was taken to Century City Hospital, arriving around 9:30 a.m. She was released two and a half hours later. Lt. Joe Lombardi of the Beverly Hills Police Department says that Love was arrested immediately after her discharge and "booked for possession of a controlled substance, possession of drug paraphernalia, possession of a hypodermic syringe and possession/receiving stolen property."

Criminal lawyer Barry Tarlow, Love's attorney, says that contrary to published reports, Love "wasn't under the influence of heroin" and "didn't overdose." He says that "she had an allergic reaction" to the tranquilizer Xanax. Tarlow says the stolen property was a prescription pad that "her doctor . . . left there when he was visiting. . . . There were no prescriptions written on it." And the controlled substance? "It was not narcotics," says Tarlow. "It's Hindu good-luck ashes, which she received from her entertainment lawyer, Rosemary Carroll."

Love was released at about 3 p.m. after posting $10,000 bail. (All charges against Love were later dropped.) She immediately checked into the Exodus Recovery Center, the same rehabilitation facility from which her husband had escaped a week earlier. The following day, April 8, she checked out when she received word that her husband had been found.

THE FIRST TIME Cobain's troubles made tabloid headlines was in August 1992, after *Vanity Fair* published an article in which its writer, Lynn Hirschberg, reported that Love had used heroin while pregnant with Frances Bean. (Love has denied this.) As a result of subsequent media attention, Love and Cobain were not allowed to be alone with their newborn daughter for one month.

After a long and taxing battle with children's services in Los Angeles, where they were then living, the couple regained custody of the girl. In a September 1992 *Los Angeles Times* article, Cobain admitted to "dabbling" in heroin and detoxing twice in the past year – a strategic move, according to an insider, to mollify children's services. In subsequent interviews, Cobain never admitted to using heroin after he and Love had detoxed before Frances Bean was born.

In the spring of 1993, after the band had recorded *In Utero* with producer Steve Albini in Minnesota, another frightening series of events began to unfold. First came good news: On March 23, 1993, following a Family Court ruling in Los Angeles, children's services stopped its supervision of Love and Cobain's child rearing. But just six weeks later, on May 2, Cobain came home (then in Seattle's Sand Point area) shaking, flushed and dazed. Love called 911. According to a police report, Cobain had taken a large dose of heroin. As Cobain's mother and sister stood by, Love injected her husband with buprenorphine, an illegal drug that can be used to awaken someone after a heroin overdose. She also gave Cobain a Valium, three Benadryls and four Tylenol tablets with codeine, which caused him to vomit. Love told the police this kind of thing had happened before.

A month later, on June 4, the police arrived at the Cobain home again after being summoned by Love. The two had been fighting over Cobain's drug use, a source says Cobain later told him. Love told the police, however, that she and Cobain had been arguing over guns in the house. Cobain was booked for domestic assault (he spent three hours in jail), and three guns found at the house were confiscated. One of those weapons, a Taurus .380, had been loaned to Cobain by Carlson. (Cobain picked up the guns a few months later; they were again confiscated in the March 1994 domestic dispute.)

Seven weeks later, on the morning of July 23, Love heard a thud in the bathroom of the New York hotel where the couple was staying. She opened the door and found Cobain unconscious. He had overdosed again. Nevertheless, Nirvana performed that night at the Roseland Ballroom. Fans never knew the difference.

A few days later, Cobain returned to Seattle. One friend says: "He just kept to himself. Every time he came back after a tour, he would get more and more reclusive. The only people that saw him a lot were Courtney, Cali and Jackie [Farry, a former baby sitter and assistant manager]."

Though, according to Gold Mountain, Cobain's clinical depression had been diagnosed as early as high school, the singer never seemed to fully believe he had a problem. "Over the last few years of his life," says Goldberg, "Kurt saw innumerable doctors and therapists."

Many who were close to Cobain remember that the musician frequently suffered dramatic mood swings. "Kurt could just be very outgoing and funny and charming," says Butch Vig, who produced *Nevermind*, "and a half-hour later he would just go sit in the corner and be totally moody and uncommunicative." "He was a walking time bomb, and nobody could do anything about it," says Goldberg.

On Sept. 14, *In Utero* was released. Even though Cobain had vowed not to "go on any more long tours" unless he could keep his chronic stomach pain from acting up, the band hit the road for a long stretch of U.S. dates. According to sources, Cobain detoxed from heroin before the tour.

On Jan. 8, 1994, Nirvana performed what would be their last American show, at the Seattle Center Arena. The band then spent the next couple of weeks relaxing in Seattle. During that time, in a move considered uncharacteristic by many, Cobain authorized Geffen to make a few changes to *In Utero*. In order to get chains such as Kmart and Wal-Mart to carry the album, which the stores had previously rejected, Geffen decided to

remove Cobain's collage of model fetuses from the back cover.

Geffen also changed the song title "Rape Me" to "Waif Me," a name that Cobain picked, according to Ray Farrell of Geffen's sales department. "At first, Kurt wanted to call it 'Sexually Assault Me,' " Farrell says, "but it took up too much room. In the end he decided on 'Waif Me' because *waif*, like *rape*, is not gender specific. *Waif* represents somebody who is at the mercy of other people." The altered version was also shipped to Singapore – the only country where *In Utero* was banned.

NIRVANA (minus Pat Smear, who was still at home in Los Angeles) emerged from hibernation on the weekend of Jan. 28 and spent three days in the studio. On Feb. 2, the band members left for Europe. They stopped in France to appear on a TV show and began their tour in Lisbon, Portugal, on Feb. 6. It was the first time Nirvana had scheduled so many consecutive dates in Europe. The band and crew traveled by bus. Cobain and Smear traveled in one bus; Grohl and Novoselic rode in another. According to road manager Alex Macleod, two buses were a matter of luxury, not animosity.

"The shows went really well," recalls Macleod. "But Kurt was tired. I mean, we were traveling a lot."

About 10 to 12 days into the tour, heading back through France, Cobain began to lose his voice. For a while, a throat spray purchased in Paris and administered before shows helped ease his discomfort.

While Nirvana was in Paris – a week before Cobain's 27th birthday – photographer Youri Lenquette witnessed a chilling scene. Cobain showed up for a photo shoot for the French magazine *Globe* and struck up different poses with a sports pistol he had recently purchased. On one occasion, Cobain foreshadowed his own suicide by pressing the gun against his temple, pretending to squeeze the trigger and miming the impact of the gunshot to his head.

After a swing through a handful of French and Italian cities – including Rome – Nirvana performed in Ljubljana, in the former Yugoslavia, on Feb. 27 and, two days later, at Terminal Einz, in Munich, Germany. It would be Nirvana's final show. Cobain lost his voice halfway through the performance and, says Macleod, went to see an ear, nose and throat specialist the next day. "[Cobain] was told to take two to four weeks' rest," Macleod says. "He was given spray and [medicine] for his lungs because he was diagnosed as having severe laryngitis and bronchitis."

According to Macleod, the doctor who prescribed the throat spray to Cobain told him: " 'You shouldn't be singing the way you're singing,' the same as they always say. 'You have to take at least two months off and learn to sing properly.' And he was like 'Fuck that.' "

The band postponed two more German shows – in Munich and Offenbach – until April 12 and 13 and took a rest. Novoselic flew back to Seattle the following day to oversee repair work on his house; Grohl stayed in Germany to participate in a video shoot for the film *Backbeat* (he played drums on the soundtrack); and Cobain and Smear headed for Rome. The band had made it through 15 shows with another 23 to go.

Cobain decided to stay in Europe. The plane trip and jet lag were too much to take in his condition. "He as much as anyone else was

bummed out that they had to pull these two shows," says Macleod. "But there was no way that he could have gone on the next night."

On March 3, Cobain checked into Rome's five-star Excelsior Hotel. That same day, in a London hotel room, a writer for the British monthly *Select* was interviewing Love, who was preparing for an English tour with Hole. The writer says that during their talk, Love was popping Rohypnol, a tranquilizer manufactured by Roche, which also makes Valium. According to pharmacists, the drug is used to treat insomnia. It has also been used to treat severe anxiety and alcohol withdrawal and as an alternative to methadone during heroin withdrawal. (Gold Mountain denies withdrawal as an issue in Love's and Cobain's cases.) Known in some parts of Europe as Roipnol, the drug is not available in the United States. "Look, I know this is a controlled substance," Love said in the interview. "I got it from my doctor. It's like Valium."

According to Gold Mountain, Love, Frances Bean and Cali met Cobain in Rome the next afternoon. That evening, Cobain sent a bellboy out to fill a prescription for Rohypnol. In an uncharacteristic move, Cobain also ordered two bottles of champagne from room service. ("He never drank," his friends confirm.)

At 6:30 the following morning, Love found Cobain unconscious. "I reached for him, and he had blood coming out of his nose," she told *Select* in a later interview, adding, "I have seen him get really fucked up before, but I have never seen him almost eat it." At the time, the incident was portrayed as an accident. It has since been revealed that some 50 pills were found in Cobain's stomach. Rohypnol is sold in tinfoil packets; each pill must be unwrapped individually. A suicide note was found at the scene. Gold Mountain still denies that a suicide attempt was made. "A note was found," says a company spokesperson, "but Kurt insisted that it wasn't a suicide note. He just took all of his and Courtney's money and was going to run away and disappear."

Cobain was rushed to Rome's Umberto I Polyclinic Hospital for five hours of emergency treatment and then transferred to the American Hospital just outside the city. He awoke from his coma 20 hours later and immediately scribbled his first request on a note pad: "Get these fucking tubes out of my nose." Three days later, he was allowed to leave the hospital. Cobain's doctor, Osvaldo Galletta, says that the singer was suffering "no permanent damage" at the time.

"He's not going to get away from me that easily," Love later said. "I'll follow him through hell."

The couple then returned to Seattle. "I saw [Kurt] the day he got back from Rome," says Carlson. "He was really upset about all the attention it got in the media." Carlson didn't notice anything abnormal about Cobain's health or behavior. Like many of Cobain's friends, he regrets that neither Cobain nor anyone close to Cobain told him that Rome had been a suicide attempt.

Sonic Youth guitarist and longtime Nirvana supporter Lee Ranaldo, who, like Nirvana, is managed by Gold Mountain, agrees. "Rome was only the latest installment of [those around Cobain] keeping a semblance of normalcy for the outside world," he says. "But I feel like I was good enough friends with Kurt that I could have called him up and said: 'Hey, how are you? Do you want to talk?' "

"I never knew [Cobain] to be suicidal," Mark Lanegan recalls. "I just knew that he was going through a really tough time."

THE DAYS after Cobain's death were filled with grief, confusion and finger pointing for all concerned. "Everyone who feels guilty, raise your hand," Love told MTV the morning after Cobain was found. She said she was wearing Cobain's jeans and socks and carrying a lock of her husband's blond hair. According to Gold Mountain, a doctor was summoned to stay with Love at all times.

"She's a strong enough person that she can take it," says Craig Montgomery, who was scheduled to manage a since-canceled spring tour for Hole.

"It was hard to imagine Kurt growing old and contented," adds Montgomery. "For years, I've had dreams about it ending like this. The thing that weirds me out is how alone and shut out he felt. It was him that shut out a lot of his friends."

Novoselic told a Seattle newspaper that he believed Cobain's death was the result of inexplicable internal forces: "Just blaming it on smack is stupid. . . . Smack was just a small part of his life." "I think drugs tampered with his life," Faith No More's Bottum agrees, "but they weren't as huge a part of his life as people make it out to be."

The news of Cobain's death was first reported on Seattle's KXRX-FM. A co-worker of Gary Smith, the electrician who found Cobain's body, called the station with what he claimed was the "scoop of the century," adding, "you're going to owe me a lot of concert tickets for this one."

"Broadcasting this information was kind of an eerie decision to make," says Marty Reimer, the on-air personality who took the call. "We're not a news station." Cobain's sister, Kim, first heard of her brother's death through radio reports, as did his mother, Wendy O'Connor. "Now he's gone and joined that stupid club," O'Connor said to a reporter, referring to Jimi Hendrix, Janis Joplin, Brian Jones and Jim Morrison. "I told him not to join that stupid club."

After Reimer called the Associated Press with the story, MTV played reruns of Nirvana's *Unplugged* performance and Seattle DJs took to the airwaves. "He died a coward," barked one Seattle DJ on KIRO-FM, "and left a little girl without a father."

"I don't think any of us would be in this room tonight if it weren't for Kurt Cobain," Pearl Jam's Eddie Vedder told a capacity audience during a Washington, D.C., concert the night that Cobain's death was announced. Vedder left the crowd with the admonition: "Don't die. Swear to God."

Outside Cobain's Seattle house the afternoon after his body was found, 16-year-old Kimberly Wagner sat on a wall for four hours, crying and fielding queries from news-hungry TV stations and magazines. "I just came here to find an answer," she sobbed. "But I don't think I'm going to."

Nearby, Steve Adams, 15, stood with a friend. As a Gray Line tour bus full of curiosity seekers passed by, he explained what Cobain's music meant to him. "Sometimes I'll get depressed and get mad at my mom or my friends, and I'll go and listen to Kurt. And it puts me in a better mood. . . . I thought about killing myself a while ago, too, but then I thought about all the people that would be depressed about it."

The Seattle Crisis Clinic received roughly 300 calls that day, 100 more than usual. Dr. Christos Dagadakis, director of emergency psychiatry at Harborview Medical Center, says, however, that "there was no particular increase in overdoses or suicide attempts coming in to our emergency room."

The following evening, on April 10, Seattle mourned Cobain as some 5,000 fans gathered in the park near the Space Needle to commemorate him. Love read excerpts from Cobain's suicide note in a taped message to the crowd, interspersing her own emotional responses to the confessions and doubts of the "sad, little, sensitive, unappreciative, Pisces, Jesus man." "I should have let him, we all should have let him have his numbness," she sobbed. "We should have let him have the thing that made him feel better."

It wasn't until hours after this candlelight vigil that Seattle experienced its first possible Cobain-related suicide. After returning home from the vigil, Daniel Kaspar, 28, ended his life with a single bullet.

The effects of Cobain's suicide reverberated around the globe. In Australia, a teenager committed suicide in an apparent tribute to Cobain. In southern Turkey, a 16-year-old fan of Cobain's locked herself in her room, cranked Nirvana music and shot herself in the head. Friends said she had been depressed ever since hearing about Cobain's death.

Elsewhere, on the evening of the vigil, Cobain's family scheduled a private memorial service at the Seattle Unity Church a few blocks away from the Seattle Center. There was no casket; Cobain's body was still in the custody of the medical examiners (he was later cremated). The Rev. Stephen Towles began the service by telling some 150 invited guests: "A suicide is no different than having our finger in a vise. The pain becomes so great that you can't bear it any longer."

Novoselic delivered a short eulogy afterward. "We remember Kurt for what he was: caring, generous and sweet," he said. "Let's keep the music with us. We'll always have it, forever." Carlson read verses from a Buddhist poet. Love, clad in black, read passages from the Book of Job and some of Cobain's favorite poems from Arthur Rimbaud's *Illuminations*. She told anecdotes about Cobain's childhood and read from his suicide note. She included parts that she had not read on tape for the vigil. "I have a daughter who reminds me too much of what I used to be," Cobain had written.

Gary Gersh, who signed Nirvana when he was with Geffen (he is now president of Capitol Records), read a faxed eulogy from Michael Stipe. Last to speak was Danny Goldberg. "I believe he would have left this world several years ago," Goldberg said, "if he hadn't met Courtney."

When the service ended, Love headed to the Seattle Center nearby, where the vigil had just ended. Fans were burning flannel shirts, shouting for Nirvana music (which they got) and taunting the police, who were trying unsuccessfully to keep them out of the public fountain. Love mingled almost unnoticed in the sea of mourners, clutching her husband's suicide note in her hand. She disappeared and then reappeared with an armload of Cobain's old clothes and possessions, which she distributed to his fans. She described herself to bystanders as "angry" and emotionally "messed up."

Kim Warnick of the local group Fastbacks surveyed the scene with KNDD-FM music director Marco Collins, who had helped organize the mass memorial. "He would have loved this," she told him. "All these kids," Collins replied, as he surveyed the undernourished teens with dyed hair, troubled eyes and torn jeans milling around him, "they look like they came from his world."

AS OF THIS WRITING, neither Grohl nor Novoselic has told his story to the press, though they have resumed making music. On July 12, at the Yoyo a Go Go festival, in Olympia, Wash., they performed together publicly for the first time since Nirvana's March 1 Munich show. Unannounced, they appeared as part of the backing band for Simon Fair Timony, a 10-year-old singer who fronts the band the Stinky Puffs (which includes his mother, Sheenah Fair, his stepfather, Jad Fair, and guitarist Don Fleming). The group performed Timony's tribute to Cobain called "I'll Love You Anyway." (Cobain, who'd nurtured Timony's interest in music since he was 6, had agreed to collaborate on an upcoming Stinky Puffs record.)

Novoselic and Grohl have also been in a Seattle studio reviewing performance tapes that will comprise a live album, possibly for a Fall 1994 release. The two are setting up, along with Cobain's family and Gold Mountain Entertainment, a scholarship fund for Aberdeen, Wash., high-school students with "artistic promise regardless of academic performance."

Children's services departments in both Seattle and Los Angeles confirmed that they had no case workers assigned to Frances Bean. Though Cobain did have a will, it was unsigned and therefore invalid at the time of his death. With no will, Love and Frances Bean have become the only heirs to his estate (which includes assets of over $1.2 million and debts of less that $740,000). Love, meanwhile, donated all of Cobain's guns, including the one he used to kill himself, to Mothers Against Violence in America; the organization had the guns melted down.

Love spent time holed up in Seattle for a while before flying to New York, where she went on a lingerie shopping spree. After Love returned to Seattle, another tragedy unfolded around her. Kristen Pfaff, the bassist in Hole, was preparing to move from Seattle to Minneapolis on the evening of June 15 when she locked herself in her bathroom around 9:30 p.m. The following morning, Paul Erickson, the bassist in the Minneapolis band Hammerhead, who had spent the night at the house, found her slumped over the side of the tub, kneeling in five inches of water. Police say they found "syringes and what appeared to be narcotic paraphernalia" in a purse on the bathroom floor. The medical examiner later reported that she died from an overdose of opiates.

"It was an accident," Hole drummer Patty Schemel told a Seattle newspaper afterward. "She loved life, and this shouldn't have happened."

Love communicated her grief on the computer bulletin board America On-Line, where she had been engaging in an active discourse with fans, friends and enemies for several weeks. "Pray for [Kurt] and Kristen," she wrote. "They hear it, I know. . . . My friend has been robbed of her stellar life. My baby has no dad. . . . Thank you for respecting the finest man who ever lived, that he loved a scum like me is testament enough to his empathy." ☻

A Cry in the Dark

The following is a transcript of Courtney Love's taped message, which includes her reading of parts of Kurt Cobain's suicide note, played to the crowd gathered for a hastily organized memorial at the Seattle Center on April 10, 1994.

I DON'T REALLY KNOW what to say. I feel the same way you guys do. If you guys don't think that I had to sit in this room when he played guitar and sing – I feel so honored to be near him – you're crazy. Anyway, he left a note. It's more like a letter to the fucking editor. I don't know what happened. I mean, it was gonna happen. It could have happened when he was 40. He always said he was going to outlive everybody and be 120. I'm not going to read you all the note, because it's none of the rest of your fucking business, but some of it is to you. I don't really think it takes away his dignity to read this, considering that it's addressed to most of you. [*Deep breath*] He's such an asshole. I want you all to say *asshole* really loud. [Everyone yells, "*Asshole!*"]

Kurt says: "This note should be pretty easy to understand. All the wording's from the Punk Rock 101. Over the years, it's my first introduction to the, shall we say, ethics involved with independence, and the embracement of your community has proven to be very true. I haven't felt the excitement of listening to as well as creating music, along with really writing for too many years now. I feel guilty beyond words about these things. For example, when we're backstage and the lights go out and the manic roar of the crowd begins, it doesn't affect me the way in which it did for Freddie Mercury [*laughs*], who seemed to love and relish in the love and admiration from the crowd" – Well, Kurt, so fucking what? Then don't be a rock star, you asshole – "which is something I totally admire and envy. The fact is, I can't fool you, any one of you. It simply isn't fair to you or to me. The worst crime I can think of would be to rip people off by faking it and pretending as if I'm having 100 percent fun." No, Kurt, the worst crime I can think of is for you to just continue being a rock star when you fucking hate it and just fucking stop. "Sometimes I feel as if I should have a punch-in time clock before I walk out onstage. I've tried everything within my power to appreciate it, and I do. God, believe me, I do. But it's not enough. I appreciate the fact that I and we have affected and entertained a lot of people. I must be one of those narcissists who only appreciate things when they're gone. I'm too sensitive." [*Sarcastically*] Aw. "I need to be slightly numb in order to regain the enthusiasm I had as a child. On our last three tours I've had a much better appreciation for all the people I've known personally and as fans of our music. But I still can't get over the frustration, the guilt and the empathy I have for everyone. [*Crying*] There's good in all of us, and I simply think I love people too much" – So why didn't you just fucking stay? – "so much that it makes me feel too fucking sad. The sad, little, sensitive, unappreciative, Pisces, Jesus man." Oh, shut up, bastard. "Why don't you just enjoy it? I don't know."

Then he goes on to say personal things to me that are none of your damn business, personal things to Frances that are none of your damn business. "I have it good, very good, and I'm grateful. But since the age of 7, I've become hateful toward all humans in general only because it seems so easy for people to get along and have empathy – Empathy! – only because I love and feel sorry for people too much, I guess. Thank you all from the pit of my burning, nauseous stomach [*crying*] for your letters and concern during the past years. I'm too much of an erratic, moody baby, and I don't have the passion anymore, so remember" – And don't remember this, because this is a fucking lie – "it's better to burn out than to fade away." [*Sighs*] God, you asshole.

"Peace, love, empathy,

"Kurt Cobain"

Then there's some more personal things that are none of your damn businesses. And just remember, this is all bullshit. But I want you to know one thing: That '80s tough-love bullshit – it doesn't work. It's not real. It doesn't work. I should have let him, we all should have let him, have his numbness. We should have let him have the thing that made him feel better, we should have let him have it, instead of trying to strip away his skin. You go home, and you go tell your parents, "Don't you ever try that tough-love bullshit on me, because it doesn't fucking work." That's what I think, when I'm laying in our bed [*sobbing*], and I'm really sorry, and I feel the same way you do. [*Sobbing harder*] I'm really sorry, you guys. I don't know what I could have done. I wish I'd have been here, and I wish I had listened to other people, but I didn't. Every night I've been sleeping with his mother, and I wake up in the morning, I think it's him, because her body's sort of the same. And I have to go now. Just tell him he's a fucker, OK? Just say, "Fucker, you're a fucker," and that you love him. ◖

News Flash, News Fade

THE WORD ON KURT COBAIN in the days before he killed himself was so awful that every time a Nirvana song came on the radio, I was sure it was only a prelude to the announcement that he was dead. Over and over, for some reason, before the fact, the song was always "Come As You Are." As it played, on Wednesday or Thursday, it seemed to slow down and expand, to drag itself across its own sound, to rub itself raw.

When the news came, the version I got was queer, ugly – mocking, not like the announcement of any other pop death. Several people were talking on KALX-FM, the Berkeley, Calif., college station. They were back-announcing records by the Raincoats and the Vaselines: ". . . two of his favorites. Yeah, it's too bad about Kurt Cobain's passing" – that moronic euphemism – "but what the hell, it's *his* life." Someone snickered, and then a loud, hyped-up tabloid voice hit the mike: *"He shot himself! With a shotgun! In a cabin next to his house! He left a note!"* "Hey," said the first voice, sarcasm dripping, "we're not making *fun* of this." They went straight into "My Way" by Sid Vicious.

That night I dreamed about a Kurt Cobain funeral procession, with an open hearse trundling the coffin down First Avenue in Seattle as thousands lined the street. Every few moments, someone would break out of the crowd, leap onto the hearse like a mosh-pit dancer taking the stage; he would lift the lid on the coffin and rush back to the sidewalk, shouting: "No face, man! No face!"

At a small gathering at Booksmith's, on Haight Street, in San Francisco, the night before Kurt Cobain's body was found, the subject of Nirvana came up. Gina Arnold, who wrote the book *Route 666: The Road to Nirvana*, spoke bitterly: "People talk about Kurt Cobain's wonderful sense of irony. There isn't any irony."

Driving for six hours from Kansas City, Mo., to Fayetteville, Ark., on Sunday, the day after the story was front page all over the country, there wasn't any Kurt Cobain. Radio today is now so demographically segmented its formats are absolutely resistant to events in the world at large. Here it's always . . . whenever it is. On Your Favorite Oldies, Best of the '70s, Lite Rock, not to mention country, adult-contemporary or hip-hop stations, Kurt Cobain didn't die, and neither was he ever born. Finally, just over the Missouri-Arkansas border, on a weird station that mixed Michael Bolton, Salt-n-Pepa and Beck, up came a no-comment "All Apologies." Probably it had been computer-programmed the week before.

It was appropriate, of course. Kurt Cobain wrote too damn many appropriate songs for suicide. Not murder, though, or anything like it – listen. The violence is always an echo; it's loud only to the one who's shouting. "Sometimes," said guitarist Roy Buchanan, another suicide, "it gets so quiet you could fire a gun inside yourself" – and, he must have meant, no one would hear it.

Was it easy to hear Kurt Cobain, as he made hits full of violence, as he struggled through that sound to do and say those things he thought were right, to stand up to and condemn those who, like Axl Rose, he believed were thugs? In that struggle, if you listened, you could almost hear a belief that to embrace decency in the world at large – to fight homophobia, to aid the suffering, to denounce evil – would be, even if your own soul were a charnel house, to find decency in yourself. Come as you are – when you live your life in pieces, it's easier said than done. The song plays in my head now, with an added line from Laurie Anderson: Come as you are, and pay as you go.

--- GREIL MARCUS

One of Them

SOMETIME BEFORE TWILIGHT on Tuesday, April 5, Kurt Cobain sat alone in the room above the garage of his home near Lake Washington, meticulously laid a piece of identification on the floor next to his body and, with a single shotgun blast to the head, ended his life at the age of 27. It was an action that occurred in the instant it takes to twitch one finger, a last act ensuring that Cobain's complex and contradictory biography will be punctuated only with question marks. In life, Cobain pleaded that he not be held up as a representative or spokesperson for anything other than himself. In death, this wish should be respected.

Born into a generation that doesn't want heroes but simply someone who understands, Cobain understood. Even his suicide note ended with "Peace, love, empathy." Yes, he was a remarkably gifted songwriter and singer, but he was special not so much because he was unique but because he was one of many. Disenfranchised and cynical. Awkward and unsure. For an enormous collection of individuals, Cobain's passing is the equivalent of a death in the family. He wasn't a hero or a guru of any sort. He was simply one of them, someone who grasped what they were going through, even though he was powerless to control these forces in his own life.

"Since the age of 7, I've become hateful toward all humans in general only because it seems so easy for people to get along and have empathy . . . only because I love and feel sorry for people too much, I guess."
– from the suicide note of Kurt Cobain

--- CHRIS MUNDY

He Screamed Out Our Angst

I CAN'T RECALL exactly where I was when I heard the news that John Lennon had been shot. I just remember feeling an overall shock and sadness in the air and also feeling that something terribly wrong had happened. But beyond that, I didn't really feel it; I didn't know him well enough to. I was 15 years old, and his songs were already being played on Muzak stations. He was someone who had represented peace, love and a decade I was too young to remember, yet he died a violent death. It was all so symbolic.

Kurt Cobain of Nirvana is the first pop icon of mine to die tragically. He took his life in a very non-rock star way – with a 20-gauge shotgun. I suppose that, too, will be symbolic to future generations, maybe as some meaningful anti-statement from the spokesman of Generation X. But right now, it feels so much more personal than that. Cobain's death hurts.

He meant something to me individually, as he did to the thousands of other depressed callers who flooded the phone lines of radio stations right after the news got out. There's a sense of loss that goes beyond just the departure of a great artist. From every unpolished crack in Cobain's voice to the frequent blemishes on his face, he was real, someone I could identify with. He conveyed the same crushed

idealism, bruised sensitivity and abrasive sarcasm I feel, and like me, he didn't smile a lot, wasn't perky or outgoing and sometimes left the house in the clothes he slept in. Kurt Cobain was the first one of my generation able to break into the Whitney Houston-dominated mainstream while never shedding his skin for a more upbeat one along the way. He sang of things *we* cared about.

My oldest sister laughs and says, "How can you understand what he sings?" But Cobain's railing screams and blurred delivery were as big a part of the emotion he conveyed as his words were — the sarcastic tilt of "Smells Like Teen Spirit" and the raging, mad tones of injustice in "Rape Me."

In his lyrics, simple lines like "Everything is my fault/I'll take all the blame" in "All Apologies" and the declaration of "I'm not like them, but I can pretend" in "Dumb" were not grandiose but instead self-deprecating and human.

I interviewed Kurt just before Nirvana hit it big with their second album, *Nevermind*, in 1991. He wasn't nodding out in a drug stupor or curled up in an antisocial ball. Instead he was articulating his feelings, ones that I had heard coming from so many of my friends. I supposed our reference points were the same; he was 24, I was only two years older. But I also got a rare sense of insight and compassion from him that superseded any generational tie. It was that quality that made Nirvana's music all the more meaningful.

"He must have truly felt what he sang," one TV journalist said while picking apart Nirvana's songs for clues to Cobain's misery. Why is it surprising he meant what he sang? Cobain's death wasn't that of a decadent rock star but instead of a 27-year-old who had problems beyond the ones we saw.

Brainstorming by all the record companies in the nation combined couldn't have concocted a more perfectly imperfect singer or songwriter. Music and lyrics that powerful can't be feigned; there has to be some validity behind them.

Cobain's and Nirvana's realism cracked the calculated veneer that waxed over rock in the '80s with *Nevermind*. It sold 10 million copies. The band brought society's undercurrents of rage to the mainstream via their own angst, and Cobain shattered the idea of what a rock star is supposed to be. Rock stars are slick and posturing; he slouched and rarely brushed his hair. He made punk rock work more than 12 years after its birth.

The '60s is an era that my peers and I are constantly reminded we missed. A great time when teens were filled with good vibes and didn't blow each other away over a pair of Adidases. They were blessed with naiveté and denial — they believed all things could be good if you tried hard enough.

Kurt Cobain was one among a league of kids raised by '60s-generation parents who shuttled their children from relative to relative in a quest for personal freedom. Courtney Love (Cobain's widow) of Hole, Billy Corgan of Smashing Pumpkins, Trent Reznor of Nine Inch Nails and Moby are just a few more. They suffered the fallout of free love, and as adults, they sell millions of albums to peers who can relate to their rootless anger and dysfunction.

I can't tell you what Kurt was thinking, though, or how he was feeling. Not all of Generation X has straight lines into one another. But I can tell you I knew something would happen to end him. Not because I saw Kurt as some sort of tragic figure, but because my cynicism tells me all good things will end. Hope is something you trick yourself with to get through the true hopelessness of life.

I will always remember where I was when the news of Kurt's death reached me. Now, like my mom with President Kennedy or my father with Anwar Sadat, I, too, have a moment etched in my mind.

--- LORRAINE ALI

Critics always stand on the edges of whatever world they love: We're the ultimate nerds, nervously standing alone at the party, concocting furious internal monologues as the revelers keep the scene in motion. This position blesses us with the need to make our voices singular, to develop insight and powerful dreams. But it doesn't make us very comfortable people,

Neve

and at the scene of a disturbance of such magnitude as
Kurt Cobain's death, this
awkwardness magnifies.
Who would want this job,
anyway; squirming in on a
community in pain, look-
ing for nasty details and
quotable quotes? The presence of cash-wielding TV-
tabloid types only made me
and the other rock writers
present feel even more
like reluctant rubberneckers.

more

Yet I don't buy the argument that a really ethical, dedicated follower of Kurt Cobain's work would have necessarily chosen silence in response to his sphinxian act. My job is a form of thinking out loud; the skill of it lies in connecting my own visions with the patterns of the world in which I live. I don't claim to have any handle on Kurt's truth or anyone else's, but I do feel that as someone who shares some of the ideals he expressed in his work, I have a responsibility to try and tell the story that involves both him and me; not the secret Kurt Cobain, but the one that was created in part by himself, in part through his community and in part by the public who embraced his work and struggled to understand his persona. All I could do was share whatever understanding I could fathom with others who might be searching for a narrative to contain the grief and horror of this death of someone who seemed like both a total stranger and an intimate friend. And so I went home, myself a stranger now, and stood on a lot of edges and reported back.

PEOPLE COULDN'T BELIEVE the photograph. The day after Kurt Cobain shot himself faceless in his million-dollar home, his friends and the hundreds of rosy, downcast kids who mourned him found a nasty slice of evidence on the front page of the *Seattle Times*: a shot taken from above the glass doors of the garage where Cobain died, revealing the suicide scene. Two detectives hover like shadows. But what's cruelly fascinating is the body. The image is only a fragment: one dirty-jean-clad leg with a white sock and a badly tied Converse, one arm from the elbow down in a light blue thrift-store shirt, one clenched fist. Near a detective's foot, another photograph can almost be seen, an official snapshot on a driver's license. The body and the license, both so small they don't seem real, feel unknowable, the definition of not enough.

"That picture was so tacky, I was shocked," says Kim Warnick on Sunday afternoon, as she bides her time until five, when the candlelight vigil would begin. Warnick fronts the longtime Seattle band the Fastbacks, and she works as a sales rep at Nirvana's former label, Sub Pop; we're discussing the media frenzy, the possible motives, the usual stuff. "But you know what really got me about it? His ID. You can see his wallet opened up to his driver's license, right by his body. Kurt didn't want any mistakes about what he was doing. He wanted to be perfectly clear."

It's a strange bit of the typical that Kurt Cobain would worry that killing himself with a shotgun was an act that might be misinterpreted. Suicide, especially one as violent as Cobain's, is the loudest possible invocation of silence; it's a perfectly clear way of turning your life into a mystery. His commitment to contradiction got him in the end, but even as he cut himself off forever, he was trying to make himself speak.

The Death

Here are some facts: Kurt Cobain, 27, singer-guitarist-writer for the world's most successful "alternative" band and Seattle's current favorite non-native-born Native Son, killed himself Tuesday, April 5, at his home near Lake Washington. He was the first rock star to commit suicide at the top of his game. His body was discovered by electrician Gary Smith three days later. Cobain is survived by an angry widow, Hole singer-songwriter Courtney Love, and a 20-month-old daughter, Frances Bean, as well as his divorced parents, band mates and various friends in the local and national music scenes. Immediately before his suicide, he had fled from a Southern California drug-treatment facility; his path up the coast to death is unclear.

A month before his death, Cobain had been hospitalized in Rome after entering a coma brought on by a mix of alcohol and prescription drugs. Shortly after that, Love called the police to Cobain's and her home because, she claimed, he was trying to kill himself. The police found four guns and 25 boxes of ammo on the premises. Four days before his body was found, Cobain's mother, Wendy O'Connor, filed a missing-person's report with the Seattle police. After his death, O'Connor was quoted as saying, "I told him not to join that stupid club," a media favorite later surpassed by the last words of Cobain's suicide note, "I love you, I love you."

And now, here are some rumors, flickering around and beyond the facts: Kurt Cobain killed himself because Courtney had finally given up on him and was filing for divorce. Courtney had been in Los Angeles or even Seattle the day before Kurt's death, not London, as reported. Cobain had spent at least one of his last nights at his and Courtney's country house with an unidentified companion. The band had broken up at least a week before the death. He'd never really kicked heroin; the supposedly accidental overdose in March was actually a suicide attempt. He killed himself because of writer's block.

There are other facts and other rumors. And then there is the wall. It's made of friends' grief, fans' confusion, journalists' embarrassment and what several writers call a "veil of silence" created by Gold Mountain, Nirvana's and Hole's management company. Above all, it builds off the special Northwest penchant for keeping things in. The wall looks like another photograph of Kurt, this one torn into pieces and pasted back together, nothing left intact or clear.

"Kurt Cobain is not a person," says Daniel House, owner of Seattle independent-record label C/Z. "He's turned into something that represents different things for different people. I understand the press is going to be all over it, but I wish they would leave it alone completely. Because that attention is why Kurt died. He had no life, no peace, constant chaos. He had become a freak."

House's view, which was duly cited in *Time* magazine the Monday after Cobain's death, is very popular in Seattle: Kurt had his troubles, but if his band had never exceeded normal expectations, like maybe headlining the 1,000-seat Moore Theatre once a year, he could have been saved.

In our century, "fame kills" is almost a mantra; add Cobain's name to the pantheon, and sign him up for a page in *Hollywood Babylon*. But it's hard, especially in a hometown, to pinpoint the moment when a star like Cobain slips into that nether realm, becomes flat and reproducible, something read instead of someone known. And Cobain spent his short career pulling away from this transformation, jumbling his statements, turning his back. For most stars, even the tragic ones, the transformation magnifies; for Cobain, it worked as erasure.

His death can be viewed as the final step on a chain of denials that are echoed in the story of his adopted town, his scene, his generation, every one radically unwilling to speak for itself. So it's no surprise that in the days following Cobain's death, nobody emerges to speak for them. Even the journalists hesitate in the face of such grief-benumbed wordlessness.

"IT'S A MUCH DIFFERENT THING HERE, with the rock scene," says Sub Pop publicist Nils Bernstein about the process of mourning. "It's one thing to suffer these losses on your own and another to do it with MTV in your face. People who didn't know Kurt feel like they did. His death is an ongoing event."

Bernstein is tired and would like to retreat to Linda's Tavern and drink a Rainier with a tight circle of friends. But in a painful coincidence, this is the Saturday long since scheduled as the date of Sub Pop's sixth-anniversary party. "Yesterday, everyone was pretty dazed," he says. "Everyone just got drunk."

They'll do the same tonight at the Crocodile Cafe, at a party that becomes a wake in a sideways manner well after the camera crews have abandoned their positions outside the windows: no speeches, no photographs held aloft, just old buddies in corners getting around to the subject gradually.

"There was a great vibe there," says Warnick the next day. "It would always come into the conversation, but everyone was very respectful of everyone else. It was really insulated very well." Warnick's right — the party felt better by far than any other moment in the weekend following Cobain's death. For a semi-outsider like me, born and raised in Seattle but now a decade gone, it felt like a welcome earned by my willingness to be cool. Scott McCaughey of the Young Fresh Fellows, Jonathan Poneman from

Sub Pop, Warnick's husband, Ken Stringfellow, of the Posies, and numerous other band members, label types and writers – all would smile, give a brief hug, murmur, "Weird day, isn't it?" and move on to more manageable subjects.

The jovial skepticism, downing another microbrew and telling a joke rather than analyzing or grieving too obviously, was pure Seattle. Native Northwesterners cultivate this say-no-more attitude, the roots of which I always identify in the historic drive toward seclusion that pushed the area's pioneers across the map. It's not the rain – it's the mountains. A full snow-capped range on either side of the municipal area. They hold us in.

Seattle's indie-rock scene reenacts, on a smaller level, the balancing act inherent in every Northwest community, whether it's as big as Seattle or as small as Cobain's native Aberdeen, between the interdependency of an isolated group and solitary individuals' preference for total self-reliance. "It's a really tight community," says one local scenester, "but when it comes right down to it, I'm not sure how much people will help each other." Her words make me think about the phrase that I've come to consider Kurt Cobain's motto, from "Radio Friendly Unit Shifter": "Hate, hate your enemies, save, save your friends." This phrase means to build a fortress around a group of like-minded people; the problems come when you find yourself at odds with your friends and thrown into contact with strangers who may or may not be enemies (and if you fear the world, it's very hard to tell).

T HE NORTHWEST'S GROWTH over the past decade, attributable partly to rock's ascendancy but mostly to the encroachment of Microsoft and other software companies, has shifted the area's balance. It's become a mecca for the young, the affluent, a forest of espresso stands and specialty boutiques. Yet at heart, it remains a company town – Cobain's death was bumped off the top of the news Saturday morning by the unveiling of Boeing's newest jet, the 777. And it retains a working-class suspicion of pretense and opportunism that's shared by the musicians and even the business people who dominate Seattle's rock world. So they find a way to stand outside themselves, as if all this success weren't happening to them, almost as if they don't want it.

"People don't let each other cross over the line, away from reality," says Ken Stringfellow, whose own fine band, the Posies, embraces pop and polish much more readily than most Seattle acts. "What makes Nirvana interesting is that they didn't have to be unrealistic to be extraordinary." Later, though, he admits that the dichotomies don't always work out so neatly. "Sometimes people's skepticism overwhelms them, and they can't enjoy what's happened."

"We lived cloistered away for so many years, and nobody gave a damn," Warnick adds. "And because of all the resources we have here, people are really against all the Guns n' Roses stuff. All that compromise."

Because of the city's growth and Seattle bands' current dominance, of course, compromise is unavoidable. But the way Seattle has become a mecca differs from the East Coast norm, in which small groups import their culture, take over a corner and slowly integrate. There are plenty of new immigrants in the Northwest, many of them Thai or Vietnamese, but the city's self-conception obscures these communities. And among the young, Seattle isn't a place where you can come as you are: You come to integrate yourself into a vision based on affinities you believe you share. For someone like Kurt Cobain, the college community of Olympia and, later, Seattle represented a chance to go inside after a childhood in the cold as a small-town outcast. And perhaps inspired by his expression, kids have flocked here to join what he sardonically called "our little tribe."

From outsider to insider, though, is always a tricky move. It's the same jump that indie rock, the music Cobain claimed lifted him from the dung heap of conformity, keeps trying to manage. Indie never really did away with rock stars – it just located them at eye level. As a young indie fan, Cobain idolized his own favorite rock bands, thought of them as the basis of his community. Just like the kids who now idolize him, he didn't perceive the gulf between artist and audience, and eventually he became part of the indie-rock elite, an elite that in many cases still denies its own elitism. But he was sensitive enough to be bothered by the distance now that he could see it between himself and the kids who thought he was lifting them out of their own shitty lives. And so he felt even more isolated.

"Kurt didn't have any friends anymore," says one old acquaintance. When people go over the edge, they've usually alienated even their most intimate companions, and at one level, this remark doesn't reflect anything beyond Cobain's particular illness. But it also makes him an indie rocker to the core, deeply troubled by that shift into broader resonance that characterizes every successful artistic act. Rich Jensen, Sub Pop's general manager, views the problem as a struggle with the sacred. "Kurt viewed his favorite bands as icons," he says. "An icon is something you own, or it's a false idol."

S EATTLE'S MUSIC COMMUNITY has been shattered by death many times in the past five years; part of the vigilant self-protectiveness I sense feels like the fear of yet another disaster. In 1990, Mother Love Bone singer Andrew Wood died of a heroin overdose. In 1991, poet and longtime scene habitué

105

Jesse Bernstein shot himself. Stefanie Sargent of 7 Year Bitch overdosed in 1992. And last July, Gits singer Mia Zapata was found strangled on a Capitol Hill side street. Wood, Sargent and Zapata were all the same age as or younger than Cobain, and because they hadn't yet reached the level of stardom that separates people from their regular lives, their deaths were, in fact, felt much more directly among local artists. They're remembered, too: Andy comes up in conversation at least four times over the weekend's course; 7 Year Bitch's soon-to-be-released C/Z album features a song about Stefanie and one about Mia. It's even called *Viva Zapata*.

"Mia's death affected all of us so much," says Matt Dresdner, bassist for the Gits, who continue to play as a three-piece; their debut album, recorded mostly before Zapata died, is out on C/Z. "She knew so many people — so many would say, 'Mia was my best friend.' Person after person, and they really felt that way. She was very accessible always and very honest."

Partly because it was a murder, Zapata's death genuinely transformed the smaller, more local scene in which she was a leading light. A women's self-defense program is now in place, and friends continue to raise money to investigate her murder. Nirvana even played one of the benefits, last fall at the King Theatre. There were also negative effects on the scene. "A lot of bands, coincidentally I imagine, broke up after she was killed," says Dresdner. "I do think Mia was a catalyst and inspired people to do stuff." Talking about Kurt with people in clubs and cafes, I actually feel his presence less than Zapata's. She is mentioned over and over. Posters asking for information adorn the wall of the Comet Tavern and Moe's; on some street corners, you can see the flyers made by friends a long time ago. There's Mia's warm, big, charming face, and the words "Damn! Damn! Damn!"

"FUCK KURT COBAIN. I can't get a job."

Gregory Askew is slumped against the side wall at the Cafe Paradiso, Capitol Hill's grooviest late-night caffeine station, the night of the announcement. The 20-year-old moved here from New Jersey a year or so ago, but he's had it with bohemian utopia. "I'm going down to Eugene, just to find a mellow town where everybody's not competing."

Askew's hardly the only kid who's unimpressed with Cobain's departure from the world; this reaction has been so common from the West Coast that the San Francisco *Examiner* did a feature on it Saturday. Like every generation of cool teens, these young fans have invented their own strange style of tuning out. They wear the clothes, play in the baby bands, hang out at all the bars and coffeehouses, all the while perfecting the art of indifference. When that

lackadaisical attitude is personified in figures like Winona and Ethan or Courtney and Kurt, the kids still look up. But they keep their glances quiet and speculative.

In Seattle, these teen-to-20-somethings are major players in moving the economy from industry to service, working in the bars and record stores they frequent, maintaining the circular flow of cash. "They're making the town what they thought it would be," says Rich Jensen as he sits alone in one of the current hot spots, a laundromat-cafe called Sit & Spin. Sub Pop's inexhaustible entrepreneurship is just one example of the attitude: You want a job? Open a store. It's indie at its most vibrant, a culture tossed up in storefronts and basement rooms.

But some kids, like Askew, remain discouraged. The recession hit Seattle a little later than the rest of the country — Boeing laid off 11 percent of its work force last year, and there were quieter adjustments at Microsoft as well — and although slacker jobs may seem unlimited, there are only so many gigs available pulling espresso. One Paradiso customer, 16-year-old Nathan Hatch, escaped from a dreary life much like the young Cobain's to find some people "even close to weird." He dropped out of school in Elma, near Aberdeen, in ninth grade and moved to Portland with a skater dude named Paul. Now he's looking for janitorial work. "I'm hopeful," he says. "But I'm pretty drunk right now."

Busy with their own anxieties, Seattle's club kids don't seem interested in making Cobain a hero. Maybe, as Nils Bernstein thinks, they're already over the mystery that not long ago fueled much of the average outcast's passion for rock & roll. "I've seen 12-year-old kids on the bus discussing record deals, dollar amounts," says Bernstein. "They know way, way, way more than they should about the industry."

If an idol demands distance, an icon wants to be put inside a devotee's pocket. The kids I found who did mourn Cobain — hovering behind police lines at the house where he'd died or building shrines from candles and Raisin Bran boxes at the Sunday-night vigil organized by three local radio stations — seemed to think of him more as a lost friend than as a candidate for that dreaded assignment: role model. In fact, they seemed a lot like he did: small, unsure, bowled over by the need to feel but worried about what to say. "When we found out, my friend Blair and I went out to our fort and just played some CDs," says Dave Johnson, a blond boy from Puyallup who's in a baby band called Thrive. "Kurt took the wimpy way out. He could have gone somewhere to gather his thoughts. I know places like that to go."

Johnson and about a dozen friends sit around a heap of flowers, votives, notes and xeroxed photographs of Kurt. The girls don't say much; they look like they're about to cry. The boys are enjoying all the chances to be interviewed. Even though it comes so awkwardly, through the death of a loved one, they tentatively embrace this moment of prominence. But they agree that like Kurt, they wouldn't be able to handle it full time.

"Being a rock star would be kinda stressful," says Johnson. "I'm not really looking for it. I'm in it for the enjoyment and fun." I wonder if he was inspired by Cobain's suicide note, which Love read to the 5,000 vigil-goers in a taped message: "I haven't felt the excitement in listening to as well as creating music . . . for too many years now. The fact is, I can't fool you, any of you." And the weary, too-wise kids in the audience really don't seem fooled.

The speakers at the vigil – a preacher, a poet, a suicide-prevention specialist – have nothing to do with why the kids were there. Even a brief taped message from Nirvana bassist Krist Novoselic seems beside the point. Only Love's statement has a visceral effect. But the weirdness of thousands of people standing around, looking at an empty stage, listening to a tape recording of a grieving widow and of the band they wouldn't hear new music from again, pushes the crowd out of its grief into an anger that soon turns playful. Near the end, a bunch of kids overrun the Seattle Center's biggest fountain, climbing on top, forming a mosh pit to no beats and no guitars. "Kurt Cobain!" they chant, then "Fuck you!" when a security guard tries to move them along, then just "Music!" Would Kurt have felt honored by this action? Well, he was a punk, he liked disruption. But the spirit that moved these kids had nothing to do with Kurt Cobain. It was simply their own spirit, the only one they feel they can trust.

A T FIRST, AFTER THE SUICIDE, Courtney Love tried to stay behind the veil – not simply out of decorum, but out of genuine grief. Courtney's been made into such a cartoon by malevolent rivals, gossip hounds and media whores that her strength in this ordeal has been, in some ways, its biggest shock. Because Courtney, who knows fakeness well enough to make it the major theme of Hole's brilliant DGC debut, *Live Through This* (scheduled to be released, in the cruelest of ironies, on April 12), refused in the end to play like a lady and did something that finally made Kurt's death – and her survival of it – seem real.

Strangely, Love performed her heroic act in absentia. The tape-recorded message she prepared for the vigil offered the weekend's only real catharsis, and not only because it bore Cobain's pathetic, soon-to-be-famous last words. What Love did was argue with him, dispute the terms of his refusal; in doing so, she opened up a view of what he must have really felt, the disorder that consumed him. She

would read a little from the note, then curse the words, then express her sorrow. "The worst crime I could think of would be to rip people off by faking it and pretending as if I'm having 100 percent fun." "No, Kurt, the worst crime I could think of is for you to just continue being a rock star when you fucking hate it. . . ." Like some heroine from Euripides, furious at the gods, Love provided some guidance to escape the dark. Some of what she said was disturbing; she's clearly not anywhere near solid ground yet. After reading the note, she revealed her own remorse. "We fucking should have let him have his numbness . . . the thing that made him feel better instead of trying to strip away his skin," she sobbed. "Just tell him he's a fucker . . . say *fucker,* you're a fucker. And that you love him." Love was the only one who made the vigil's audience cry.

As much as the loss of Nirvana, the dissolution of the Love-Cobain partnership is an artistic tragedy. These two were exploring the male-female dynamic together, as musicians and as public figures, with insight, daring and a sometimes fruitful incomprehension. Just as it's mercilessly unfair to blame Love for Cobain's death, it may be in bad taste to point out that he committed suicide the week her album was to be released. Whatever the particulars of his anger, if her career is stalled, that will also be a significant loss.

Listening to Love's tape at the vigil, I began to think about women's silence vs. men's, and the balance of power that causes women to speak when men feel they can remain silent. Powerful men can keep their words to themselves; power speaks for them. Part of Cobain's personal tragedy was his inability to feel his own power; at this moment, Love's achievement is to be able, across the black expanse of her sorrow, to maintain a sense of her own.

I N HIS PAINFUL LAST LOVE LETTER to a world he couldn't grasp, Kurt Cobain quoted Neil Young: "It's better to burn out than to fade away." "This is all bullshit," Love said to her ruined husband as she read the note aloud. Truth is, Cobain didn't even burn out. He fell out of our lives, unfinished. All the media attention – the vigil and the memorials in print and the endless rounds of *MTV Unplugged* – only recalls his absence, the lack he stood for and could never fill.

A few years ago, a friend of mine died of a heroin overdose. He'd been long gone before he actually left the earth. His old lover said Ted died because he could never find the words to say what he really wanted. Cobain's whole struggle, the same one rock's going through in its most serious moments these days, was to cut into himself until he found a vocabulary that might offer those words. Sometimes a few of them would gush forth. In the end, though, silence swallowed him alive. ◐

Hero

By Ann Powers

The Lost Boy

By Chris Mundy

KURT DONALD COBAIN was born Feb. 20, 1967, in a small town just outside the remote city of Aberdeen, Wash. He was the first child born to Donald, a mechanic, and Wendy, a homemaker who later worked as a secretary. In three years, the arrival of a sister, Kim, completed the family.

An inquisitive and energetic child, Cobain's earliest memories were exceedingly happy. He was the center of attention — singing, drawing, acting out skits at family outings. And then, in the time leading up to his eighth birthday, Cobain's world changed drastically. His mother filed for divorce, an action his father bitterly protested, to no avail. Sullen and withdrawn, Cobain lived for one year with his mother before moving in with his father.

"After the divorce he changed completely," his mother told ROLLING STONE in 1992. "I think he was ashamed. And he became very inward — he just held everything. He became really shy. It just devastated him."

Compounding the problem of his home life was the fact that this home was a trailer park in the belly of Aberdeen, a dreary logging community not known for its compassionate attitude toward delicate, artistically curious misfits. Often sickly, Cobain had been given Ritalin (a form of speed) to counteract hyperactivity as a child. Later he was diagnosed with chronic bronchitis and a mild case of scoliosis. Nevertheless, his frail frame was overshadowed by his increasingly obstinate nature. In a eulogy at Cobain's memorial service, his uncle Larry Smith recalled the story of Kurt being beaten up by a 250-pound logger. Cobain never even fought back, Smith said, smiling instead and giving his assailant the finger every time Cobain was slammed to the ground. Eventually, the logger gave up and walked away.

But just as resilience is not easily measured, not all scars are visible to the naked eye. For some people, like Cobain, they can exist in a place inside the body where screams are born.

In 1979, Cobain's family was faced with the suicide of a great-uncle of Cobain's. Five years later another uncle also committed suicide. It is clear that life in the Cobain family was not easy. When Donald Cobain remarried a woman with a son and daughter of her own, Kurt's already strained relationship with his father began to disintegrate altogether. Kurt was kicked out of the house to live with an aunt and uncle before eventually returning to his father's home. Another communication breakdown sent him packing again. And again. In all, between 1975 and 1984, Kurt lived sporadically with his father as well as with his paternal grandparents and three sets of aunts and uncles. Finally, he persuaded his mother to clear a space for him in her house. That lasted a year.

Wendy Cobain had also remarried, and the addition of an erratic son to an already shaky environment proved too great a strain. On one occasion, after finding out that her husband had cheated on her, Wendy pointed a gun at his head and threatened to kill him. Both children watched as she attempted unsuccessfully to load the weapon. Finally, in frustration, she gathered all the firearms in the house, marched into the night and threw them in the Wishkah River. The next day, after paying two kids to fish them out, Kurt sold the guns for pocket cash. He used the money to buy his first amplifier.

Meanwhile, punk rock was thriving, and punk rock sounded like Cobain felt: desperate, angry, raw. He dropped out of high school, was booted from his mother's house and bounced from one friend's couch to the back seat of the next friend's car. At one point, Cobain even lived under a bridge. He talked with his friend Krist Novoselic about forming a band and, within a couple years and a few more name changes (Fecal Matter, Skid Row), Nirvana were born.

Cobain's literal and spiritual deliverance finally came in the fall of 1987. Olympia, Wash., and Aberdeen are only 50 miles apart, but for Kurt Cobain, they were as polarized as heaven and hell. Home of Evergreen State College, an ultraliberal and artistic mecca of the Northwest, Olympia proved to be Cobain's lifelong psychic base. While he had gone there to live with his girlfriend Tracy Marander, Cobain had also discovered — for the first time in his life — a community that welcomed and appreciated his talents. He fell under the spell of Calvin Johnson, leader of the band Beat Happening and the head of K Records, the innocent, lo-fi independent label whose logo was soon tattooed on Cobain's forearm. His days in Olympia, in retrospect, were Cobain's college equivalent and the education of his lifetime. He called the friends who heeded Johnson's advice Calvinists, worked on collages and paintings and began writing and rehearsing with Nirvana in earnest.

By 1988, the group had recorded a batch of demo tapes and released its first single, "Love Buzz"/"Big Cheese," on Sub Pop Records. By 1989, their debut album, *Bleach*, proved that something different was happening. It was frightening and abrasive but possessed a quality that was eerily familiar, almost comfortable. The band toured, replaced drummer Chad Channing with Dave Grohl and readied themselves to record once again. And that's when it happened.

Nevermind was released in September of 1991 to little fanfare and even less expectation. Within months it became the first punk-rock record to ever reach No. 1, eventually selling 10 million copies worldwide. Rife with the conflicts of its songwriter, the music introduced Kurt Cobain to the world. It was violence and retreat, lashing out at the exact moment it soothed the pain. More than the message itself, it was *Nevermind*'s method that captured what its listeners were dying to express. It shrieked.

Offstage, however, Cobain was notoriously quiet. He was moody and introspective, and the actions swirling around him often spoke louder than he did.

Nirvana were changing the face of music in the '90s, and no matter how much he attempted to curl into a corner, somewhere out of the spotlight, Cobain was always at the eye of the hurricane. He developed a drug problem that would plague him until his final days. His romance with Courtney Love, lead singer of the fellow punk band Hole, left a path of debris-strewn tales that cemented their role as a modern-day Sid and Nancy. Months after the pair's Feb. 24, 1992, wedding in Hawaii and a few weeks past the Aug. 18, 1992, birth of their daughter, Frances Bean, Cobain lay on the grass next to his trailer at the MTV Video Music Awards and played with his baby. Reminded of his and Love's punk-love spree, he smiled. "I'm sorry about all that," he said. "It was kind of that silly, animalistic mating ritual kind of thing. Now I'm a dad. Everything's changed."

In reality little had. Reports that Love had used heroin during her pregnancy led to a protracted battle with the Los Angeles

A FIFTH-GRADE KURT COBAIN PLAYING DRUMS WITH HIS SCHOOL BAND, A FEW YEARS BEFORE HE SWITCHED TO GUITAR.

County Department of Child Services for custody of Frances Bean. A domestic disturbance in which police confiscated a number of guns made headlines even when Cobain's band was not making music. After releasing *Incesticide*, a compilation of singles and B sides, the band recorded *In Utero*, an inspired but less commercial follow-up to *Nevermind*. The 1993 record sat at the center of a controversy with Geffen, Nirvana's record label, over the album's production. Friends worried about his ongoing struggle to kick heroin.

But there was the music. *In Utero* debuted at No. 1. The band headlined a benefit for Bosnian rape victims, embarked on a tour and captured a brilliant performance on *MTV Unplugged* that, sadly, will serve as the group's epitaph. There were Cobain's friendships and his marriage, which despite the chaos that defined it, seemed to provide him with the truest taste of happiness and, oddly enough, peace he had ever known. And then, of course, there was Frances Bean, the beautiful daughter who shares her name with actress Frances Farmer, another child of Seattle who was haunted by fame and the clash of her own artistic vision and personal demons. Through all of his trials, his friends say, Cobain realized that his greatest gift was his daughter.

The fact that the world is weeping with his family is a testimonial to the power of Cobain's shared confusion and catharsis. No matter how much people might try to paint him otherwise, Kurt Cobain was not the reincarnation or manifestation of some other generation's idols. He was simply Kurt Cobain, a singular and paradoxical member of a generation full of singular and paradoxical individuals. He was remarkably frail yet possessed a scream so piercing that it was able to break through the radio silence facing rock & roll at the time of *Nevermind*; he was an unselfish music fan who gave as much back to his idols as they had given him; he was at times sweet, at others passively antisocial, retreating into his own skin rather than spitting in the faces of those he shunned; he was a child of divorce, a husband and a father; he was a heroin addict; he was a passionate advocate of the rights of women and homosexuals; and in the end, he is another statistic in the nation's suicide capital at a time when the suicide rate for his age group has doubled in the last 10 years.

Kurt Cobain is dead at the age of 27. He leaves behind him a wife who loved him, a daughter who will never know him and millions of strangers whose lives have been enriched because he lived. ◐

The Road from Nowhere

By Mikal Gilmore

IT IS EARLY on a rainy Saturday night in Aberdeen, Wash., and nearly everybody in this small tavern off the main drag is already drunk. Aaron Burckhard is considerably less drunk than most — he's only on his third beer — though, in truth, he has fair reason to be drinking. It has been just a little over a week since the body of his old friend Nirvana's Kurt Cobain was found in Seattle, the victim of a suicide, and Burckhard is still reeling from the news.

Burckhard, who was Nirvana's first drummer, had not spoken with or seen Cobain in some time. Though the two of them had their share of dis-agreements — which came to a head when Cobain fired Burckhard for being too hung over to show up for a rehearsal — Burckhard still had friendly feelings for his old band mate and for what he had seen Nirvana accomplish. "Kurt was the coolest person I knew, and still is," says Burckhard, staring straight into his beer glass. "I loved him."

Burckhard, who is now 30, begins to tell how he heard the news of Cobain's death on the radio — how he began shaking so violently that he had to lay his 5-month-old daughter down on the sofa next to him so that he would not drop her in his grief — when a guy in a jean jacket comes reeling through the tavern door and stumbles across the room, toppling tables in his way. He staggers to the bar, orders a beer and then sees Burckhard and edges our way. He begins telling Burckhard about a mutual friend who recently began shooting heroin again, until Burckhard, vis-ibly pissed, cuts him off: "That's just *fucked*, man. That guy just got clean. Why would he start using again?"

The other man shrugs and sips from his beer. "You're right, that shit's bad," he says. "But then, hell, I'm strung out on it right now myself." The guy in the jean jacket grips his beer and lurches to the other side of the tavern.

Burckhard shakes his head, then turns back to me. "Man, that is *so* fucked," he says. "There's been an epidemic of that shit around here lately."

Burckhard sits quietly for a few moments until his thoughts return to Cobain. "You know," he says, "I never really understood why Kurt was so *down* on this town. I mean, everybody talks about what a depressed place it is to live in, but I don't know what there is to *hate* about it. Except maybe . . . " Burckhard pauses and glances around him — at the people staring with hard and angry looks into their beer glasses. "Yeah," says Burckhard. "I don't know what there is to hate about this place. Except for, you know, the people who live here."

And then he laughs and returns to his beer.

ABERDEEN IS A HARD-HIT LUMBER TOWN locat-ed midway up Washington's outer coast and nestled at the deepest-cut point of a seaport called Grays Harbor. The town is nearly four miles wide and three miles long, and it is flanked on its northern and eastern borders by a ridge of steep hills, where the richer folks — who run the local sawmills — have traditionally lived in lovely and ornate Victorian-style homes. Below those hills is a poorer part of town called the flats, and it is there that Kurt Cobain grew up. His mother, Wendy O'Connor, still lives there in a small, greenish house with a tidy yard and drawn curtains. It is one of the better homes in the area. Many of the nearby houses are marred by faded paint and worn roofs and the necessary neglect that is the result of indigence.

COBAIN'S HOMETOWN (LEFT); WENDY O'CONNOR'S ABERDEEN HOME (ABOVE)

Stand in the heart of the flats — or in Aberdeen's nearby downtown area, where empty industrial struc-tures loom like haunted shells — and the frequent fog that pours off the rich folks' hills can feel like something that might bog you down here forever. Move to the other end of town, where the main drag, Wishkah Street, looks out toward the Chehalis River and the Pacific Ocean, and you feel like you're staring at the end of the world — that if you kept going, you would simply drop off the last edge of America.

This is the town that Kurt Cobain could never repudiate enough. It was here that he was scorned and beat upon both by those who should have loved him and by those who hardly knew him but recog-

nized his otherness and wanted to batter him for it. It was here, no doubt, where Cobain first learned how to hate life.

You wouldn't know it now, but Aberdeen was once a hopping place, supported by thriving lumber companies and dozens of the West Coast's most popular whorehouses. But the prostitution was killed off decades ago, and the lumber boom started coming to a halt a few years back as the economy fell and available lands were depleted. These days, there is widespread concern that the Northwestern logging industry can never fully recover and, as a result, that a town like Aberdeen is marked for a slow and ugly death.

To make matters worse, in the days following Kurt Cobain's suicide, Aberdeen became an object of national scrutiny and fast judgment. In large part, that's because Cobain had been outspoken in his dislike for his hometown — describing it essentially as a place of redneck biases and low intelligence. It's as if the town were being held in part accountable for Cobain's ruin — which is not an entirely unfathomable consideration. When you are confronted with the tragic loss of a suicide, you can't help sorting backward through the dead person's life, looking for those crucial episodes of dissolution that would lead him to such an awful finish. Look far enough into Kurt Cobain's life, and you inevitably end up back in Aberdeen —

the homeland that he fled. Maybe there was something damaging and ineradicable that he bore from this place and that he could not shirk or annihilate until those last few moments in that apartment above the garage of his Seattle home.

Certainly, there are some grim truths about the town that cannot be ignored. In April 1991, Aberdeen's local newspaper, the *Daily World,* ran an article chronicling the relatively high death rate in the region — especially in its suicide index. It is difficult to measure these things with any definitive accuracy, but Aberdeen's suicide rate would appear to average out to something like 27 people per 100,000 — which is roughly twice the national rate (though the town's population itself is something less than 17,000). Mix this news with high rates of alcohol and drug usage, as well as a high incidence of unemployment and domestic violence and a median household income of about $23,000, and you emerge with the unsurprising conclusion that Aberdeen can be a very depressing town to call your home.

One doesn't have to look beyond Cobain's family history to see evidence of this truth. In July 1979, one of Cobain's great-uncles, Burle Cobain, committed suicide by way of a gunshot to his abdomen. Five years later, Burle's brother Kenneth killed himself with a shot to the head. There are rumors that other relatives and ancestors also committed suicide — making for the legend that Courtney Love has referred to as the Cobain curse.

It is hard to know what impact, if any, the suicides of his great-uncles and others may have had on Cobain — whether he mourned these deaths or in fact saw in them the glimmer of a dark promise: a sure-fire prescription for release come the time that any further days of pain or torment would be unbearable. In any case, there was something clearly kindred — as well as something horribly ironic — in the manner in which the young artist chose to end his life. For all the ways that Cobain reviled what he saw as this area's redneck mentality, in the end he chose for himself the same style of death that others in his family and hometown had opted for: a gun to his head, obliterating the part of him that made him knowable to the outside world. As one friend, who had known him when he lived here, put it: "I hate to say it, but it was the perfect Aberdonian death."

T HERE IS LITTLE doubt that Kurt Cobain did not have an easy time of life in this town. He was born in nearby Hoquiam in 1967, the first child of Wendy and her auto-mechanic husband, Donald. The family moved to Aberdeen when Kurt was 6 months old, and by all accounts, he was a happy, bright child who, by the second grade, was already regarded as possessing a natural artistic talent. Then, in 1975, when Kurt was 8, Donald and Wendy divorced, and the bitter separation and its aftermath were devastating to the child. In the years that followed, Cobain was passed between his mother's home, in Aberdeen, his father's, in nearby Montesano, and sometimes the homes of other relatives in the region. (There are rumors that Cobain suffered physical abuse and exposure to drug abuse during this time, but nobody in the family was available to confirm or deny these reports.)

In short, the young Kurt Cobain was a misfit — it was the role handed to him, and he had the intelligence to know what to do with it. Like many youthful misfits, he found a bracing refuge in the world of rock & roll. In part, the music probably offered him a sense of connection that was missing elsewhere in his life — the reaffirming thrill of participating in something that might speak for or embrace him. But rock & roll also offered him something more: a chance for transcendence or personal victory that nothing else in his life or community could offer. Like many kids before him, and many to come, Kurt Cobain sat in his room and learned to play powerful chords and dirty leads on cheap guitars; he held music closer to himself than his family or home, and for a time it probably came as close to saving him as anything could. In the process, he found a new identity as a nascent punk.

T HOUGH COBAIN IS now Aberdeen's most famous native son, and though many people recall him from his time here, there's something about his presence that proves shadowy and inscrutable to the locals. Lamont Shillinger, who heads Aberdeen High School's English department, saw as much of him

as most people outside his family. For nearly a year, during the time he played music with the teacher's sons, Eric and Steve, Kurt slept on the Shillingers' front-room sofa, and in those moments when Kurt's stomach erupted in the burning pain that tormented him off and on for years, Shillinger would head out to the local Safeway and retrieve some Pepto-Bismol or antacids. But for all the time he spent with the family, Kurt remains a mystery to them. "I would not claim," says Lamont Shillinger, "that I knew him well, either. I don't think my sons knew him well. In fact, even to this day, I suspect there are very few people that really knew Kurt well — even the people around him or the people he was near to. I think the closest he ever came to expressing what was inside was in his artwork, in his poetry and in his music. But as far as personal back and forth, I seriously doubt that he was ever that close to anybody."

Another Aberdeen High teacher, Bob Hunter, affirms Shillinger's view. Hunter, who is part of the school's art department, began teaching Cobain during his freshman year and worked with him for three years. Though the two had a good relationship, Hunter can recall few revealing remarks from his student. "I really believe in the idea of aura," says Hunter, "and around Kurt there was an aura of 'Back off.' But at the same time, I was intrigued by what I saw Kurt doing. I wanted to know where he was getting the ideas he was coming up with for his drawings. You could detect the anger — it was evident even then."

Hunter lost track of Cobain for a while after Cobain dropped out of school, until he had Cobain's younger sister, Kim, in one of his classes. From time to time, Kim would bring tapes of her brother's work to the teacher and keep him informed of his former student's progress. Says Hunter: "Even if Kim had never come back and said that Kurt was really making it as a musician, I would have kept wondering about him. I've taught thousands of students now, but he would have been up there in my thoughts as one of the preeminent people that I hold in high esteem as artists. Later, after I heard the contents of his suicide note, I was surprised at the part where he said he didn't have the passion anymore. From what I had seen, I would have thought the ideas would always be there for him. I mean, he could have just gone back to being a visual artist, and he would have remained brilliant."

I N TIME, Cobain got out of Aberdeen alive — at least for a while. In 1987 he formed the first version of the band that would eventually become Nirvana, with fellow Aberdonians Krist Novoselic on bass and Aaron Burckhard on drums. A few months later, Cobain moved to Olympia and Novoselic to Tacoma; eventually Burckhard was left behind. Nirvana played around Olympia, Tacoma and Seattle and recorded the band's first album, *Bleach,* for Sub Pop in 1989. The group plowed through a couple more drummers before settling on Dave Grohl and recording its groundbreaking major-label debut, *Nevermind,* for Geffen in 1991. With *Nevermind,* Cobain forced the pop world to accommodate the long-resisted punk aesthetic at both its harshest and its smartest and did so at a time when many pundits had declared that rock & roll was effectively finished as either a mainstream cultural

or a commercial force. It was a remarkable achievement for a band from the hinterlands of Aberdeen, and the whole migration – from disrepute on Washington's coast to worldwide fame and pop apotheosis – was pulled off in an amazingly short period of time. Back at home, many of the kids and fans who had shared Cobain's perspective were heartened by the band's accomplishment.

But when Cobain turned up the victim of his own hand in Seattle on April 8, 1994, those same kids' pride and hope took a hard blow. "After the suicide," says Brandon Baker, a 15-year-old freshman at Aberdeen High, "all those jocks were coming up to us and saying stuff like 'Your buddy's dead. What are you going to do *now?*' Or: 'Hey, I've got Nirvana tickets for sale; they're half off.'"

Baker is standing along with a few of his friends in an alcove across the street from the high school where some of the misfit students occasionally gather to seek refuge from their more conventional colleagues. The group is discussing what it's like to be seen as grunge kids in the reality of post-Nirvana Aberdeen. Baker continues: "I realize that Kurt Cobain had a few more problems than we might, but him doing this, it kind of cheated us in a way. We figured, 'If someone like him could make it out of a place like this . . . .' It was like he might have paved the way for the rest of us. But now we don't want people to think that we're using his path as our guideline. It's like you're almost scared to do *anything* now. People around here view us as freaks. They see us walking together in a mall, and they think we're a bunch of hoodlums just looking for trouble. They'll throw us off the premises just for being together. I don't know – it's sad how adults will classify you sometimes."

The talk turns to the subject of the summer's upcoming Lollapalooza tour. In the last few days, the *Daily World*'s headlines have been given to coverage of a major local wrangle: The Lollapalooza tour organizers have proposed using nearby Hoquiam as the site for their Washington show, in part as a tribute to all that Cobain and Nirvana did for alternative music and the region. Many residents in the area, though, are incensed over the idea. They are worried about the undesirable elements and possible drug traffic that might be attracted by such an event, and even though the stopover would bring a big boon to the badly ailing local economy, there is considerable resistance to letting such a show happen in this area.

"You would think," says Jesse Eby, a 17-year-old junior, "that they would let us have this one thing – that the city council would realize we might appreciate or respect them more if they let something like this show come here. It would be such a good thing for the kids around here."

"Yeah," says Rebecca Sartwell, a freshman with lovely streaks of magenta throughout her blond hair. "I mean, can't we just have *one* cool thing to do, just one day out of the year? I mean, besides go to Denny's and drink coffee?"

Everybody falls silent for a few moments, until Sartwell speaks up again. "I don't know how to explain this," she says, "but all I want is *out.* Maybe I'll move to Olympia or Portland or someplace, but when I get there, I don't intend to say, 'Hey, I'm from *Aberdeen,*' because then everybody's going to assume I'm an alcoholic, manic-depressive hick. It's bad enough having to live here. I don't want to take the reputation of the place with me when I leave."

Everybody nods in agreement with Sartwell's words.

OT FAR FROM THE PLACE where Kurt Cobain's mother lives is a short span known as the North Aberdeen Bridge. It reaches across the narrow Wishkah River, leading into the part of town known as North Aberdeen. In the winter of 1985, during a time when he had no place to live, Kurt Cobain used to spend his afternoons at the local library and his nights sleeping on a friend's sofa or on the porch deck of his mother's house. Sometimes, though, he slept under the North Aberdeen Bridge, in a space up the sloping bank near the bridge's south side, just feet below the overhead pavement. I climbed under that bridge during my last rainy afternoon in Aberdeen to take a look around. There's a hollow cleared out of the brownish-red soil, close to the concrete buttresses, and it is here that Cobain slept. Indeed, there are more signs of him in this one place than any other spot in Aberdeen, outside of his mother's home. The columns and cylinders are covered by his spray-painted graffiti, bearing the names of bands like Black Flag and Meat Puppets and slogans like FUCK and STOP VANDALISM.

I sit down in the hollow in the dirt for a few minutes and stare out at the Wishkah River. From here, its water doesn't appear to flow. Rather, it just seems to stand there, stagnant and green. I hear a clatter behind me, and I turn around. A rat? The wind? I sit there, and I think what it would be like to hear that sound in the dead of a cold night, with only a small fire at best to illuminate the dark. I try to imagine what it was like to be a boy in this town and turn to the bridge as your haven. Who knows: Maybe the nights Cobain spent here were fun, drunken nights, or at least times of safety, when he was out of the reach of the town that had already harmed him many times. But in the end, I have to lapse into my own prejudices: It seems horrible that this was the kindest sanctuary a boy could find on a winter night in his own hometown.

I get up to leave, and my eye catches something scrawled on a rail overhead. It is hard to make out, but the writing looks much like the examples of Cobain's penmanship that I have seen recently in books and news articles. The scrawl reads: WELL, I MUST BE OFF. IT'S TIME FOR THE FOOL TO GET OUT.

Maybe it is indeed Cobain's writing, or maybe it's the script of another local kid who came to realize the same thing Cobain realized: To save yourself from a dark fate, you have to remove yourself from dark places. Sometimes, though, you might not remove yourself soon enough, and when that happens, the darkness leaves with you. It visits you not just in your worst moments but also in your best, dimming the light that those occasions have to offer. It visits you, and it tells you that *this* is where you are from – that no matter how far you run or how hard you reach for release, the darkness, sooner or later, will claim you.

You can learn a lot of bad things when you are made to sleep under a bridge in your homeland, and some of those things can stay with you until the day you die. ◖

You rode off in the sun but I love you anyway

SIMON TIMONY FAIR

age 10 lead singer of the Stinky Puffs

Live Through

By Michael Azerrad

AST SPRING, Kurt Cobain sat at his kitchen table at 3 a.m., chain-smoking and toying with one of the medical mannequins he collected. "It's hard to believe that a person can put something as poisonous as alcohol or drugs in their system and the mechanics can take it — for a while," he said to me, absently removing and inserting the doll's lungs, liver, heart.

At 5 feet 7 inches, 125 pounds, Kurt was slight, painfully thin; he'd wear several layers of clothes under his usual cardigan and ripped jeans just to appear a little more substantial. He knew well just how much abuse that fragile frame could withstand.

A few days after Kurt's death, a Seattle limo driver who had

often squired Kurt around town remarked: "Nice young man. Very quiet. But I guess he had a lot of hurtin'." Between stomach pain, chronic bronchitis and scoliosis, hurtin' dominated Kurt's life.

Many believed Kurt's stomach pain was just a lie to rationalize his heroin use, but it was real; his mother had identical symptoms in her mid-20s. Ironically, Kurt said his scream emanated from precisely the same spot that he felt the pain in his guts; even playing guitar was sometimes painful because of his scoliosis. But what tormented Kurt wasn't merely physical. All that talent and charisma packed into such a brittle, little package recalled Robert Fripp's description of Jimi Hendrix as a thin wire with too much current running through it.

Kurt realized fame was alienating him from his friends, whose entire creative and social lives were predicated on poverty. When he bought a Lexus earlier this year, peer pressure made him trade it back in and stick with his trusty old gray Volvo.

Indeed, friendship was a big reason Kurt stayed in the band. Krist Novoselic and David Grohl were two of the best, most loyal friends he had left. And he knew firsthand the power of the music they made together – the endorphin rush of performance erased even his most excruciating stomach pain. That's why he sometimes hurled himself into the drums during the encores – to prove that he was feeling no pain. Still, Kurt was growing apart from the

Frances was the light of Kurt's life — whenever she was around, his face would brighten, he'd flash a rare grin, and the entire room (or bus) filled with his joy.

Nirvana had resolved to make roadwork pleasant — they picked their favorite bands to open, including the Breeders, the Butthole Surfers, Chokebore, Half Japanese, Mudhoney and Shonen Knife. They indulged in two band buses, nice hotels and a masseur. They booked numerous days off and brought along wives, fiancées and friends. Maybe that's why they played the most consistently amazing concerts of their career.

Halfway through the tour, a bunch of us caught a club set by the British punk-pop legends the Buzzcocks. Backstage, the Buzzcocks told Kurt what an honor it was to meet him, but over and over he softly insisted, "No, it's an honor to meet you." Later, he hung out in front, chatting with some punk-rock kids who treated him as a peer — they didn't even ask for autographs. Kurt was very happy. Not everyone found him so approachable. Kurt's piercing eyes, his moodiness, his chemical state, his fame and his almost palpable charisma were extremely intimidating. But he was actually a kind, sweet man and a sincere listener.

I found this out when I traveled with Nirvana on that tour. By the time we reached New Orleans, in December, I was in the middle of a personal crisis. From a pay phone on Bourbon Street, I made a midnight call to Kurt, who invited me over to his hotel room to talk. He was exhausted but eager to help — he even opened up about his own history of moribund relationships and creative lulls. At 4 a.m., I was in the middle of a sentence when he just shut his eyes and drifted off to sleep. He wasn't high; he simply couldn't stay awake anymore. "Why'd you leave?" he demanded the following morning.

At tour's end, in December, Nirvana appeared on *MTV Unplugged*. Kurt chose an unprecedented number of covers, and revealingly, they were either about fame, death or both. Meat Puppets' "Plateau" says there's only more work when you reach the top, while on David Bowie's "The Man Who Sold the World," Kurt intoned, "I thought you died alone a long, long time ago." "Don't expect me to cry for all the reasons you had to die," he crooned on "Jesus Wants Me for a Sunbeam." That was the last time I saw Kurt Cobain. He hugged me goodbye.

Like most suicides, Kurt's provided plenty of hints; in retrospect, they were beyond cries for help — they were announcements. That's the way he was. "He was unhappy before he was famous, and he was unhappy after he was famous," says former Nirvana manager Danny Goldberg. "He was just unhappy."

In August 1992, Nirvana's triumphant set closed England's Reading Festival. Still wearing the doctor's smock he'd worn during the show, Kurt walked offstage hand in hand with a little boy with terminal cancer who had wangled his way backstage. Kurt slowly descended a set of stairs as one klieg light beamed down on him. All in white, his blond hair gleaming, he looked just like an angel, the boy a cherub. A crowd of people surrounded Kurt, but somehow the light never touched them. It was very quiet, especially after the thunderous noise of the show. The crowd followed him down an alleyway made by the backstage tents. Then Kurt turned a corner, still hand in hand with the boy, and was gone. ◓

thing he loved most. "I just don't feel the same, emotionally, about our music anymore," he told me, relaxing at home just after completing *In Utero*. "With this record, I'm just deadpan. My emotions just don't come out during it. I don't know if that's the production, the performance or just my lack of interest at this point."

On April 9, 1993, Nirvana played San Francisco's Cow Palace to benefit Bosnian rape victims. Kurt arrived to find a large entourage filling the dressing room, and he slouched in a folding chair against the wall. There was another chair next to him, but nobody could just plop down and talk to him. So I did. He smiled, said, "Hi," and plunked Frances onto my lap. We chatted about *Speed Racer*, one of his favorite TV shows. He sang me the theme song.

The drug rumors, still unconfirmed, were raging: Was Kurt a debilitated junkie who couldn't perform or write anymore? Was the band that had already revolutionized the music industry a flash in the pan? The show silenced the skeptics. The *Nevermind* songs were as uplifting as ever; the new material exuded undeniable power.

It seemed prosaic at the time, but hindsight says otherwise: Kurt changed what side of the stage he played on, from his usual stage left to stage right. "It kind of makes it interesting again," he explained.

In October, Nirvana began their first U.S. tour in two years. The band's new guitarist, Pat Smear, bolstered Kurt with propulsive chording and passionate leads, but he also played another crucial role: He never failed to lift Kurt's spirits. But nobody could lift those spirits quite like Kurt's daughter. Frances accompanied Kurt for most of the tour while Courtney recorded her new album.

Heart-Shaped NOISE

OMETIME DURING THE MONTHS leading up to the recording sessions for Nirvana's last album, Kurt Cobain wrote a song called "I Hate Myself and I Want to Die." It was a phrase he used a lot at the time — ever since the band's Australian tour in the winter of 1992 — as a backhanded response to people who kept asking him how he was doing. Cobain thought it was so funny he wanted it to be the title of the album.

"Nothing more than a joke," Cobain said of the song and sentiment, grinning through a thick haze of cigarette smoke as we talked in a Chicago hotel room last fall. "I'm thought of as this pissy, complaining, freaked-out schizophrenic who wants to kill himself all the time. 'He isn't satisfied with anything.' And I thought it was a funny title."

Eventually, the gag wore thin. Cobain changed the title of the album first to *Verse Chorus Verse* (a dig at cookie-cutter songwriting and his own fear of the rut), then to *In Utero*. He also yanked the song "I Hate Myself and I Want to Die" — a short, dour punker — from the record on the eve of release. As if to prove how little it all mattered by then, he eventually gave the song to those cartoon boobs Beavis and Butt-head; Cobain's joke ended up as the opening track on the otherwise witless LP *The Beavis and Butt-head Experience*.

IT NOW APPEARS there is more truth in that song than Kurt Cobain ever cared to admit.

Or is there? In the wake of Cobain's tragic suicide, his Nirvana songbook rings long and loud with the clamor of dark prophecy: "You can't fire me, because I quit" ("Scentless Apprentice"); "Everything is my fault/I'll take all the blame" ("All Apologies"); "Monkey see monkey do/I don't know why I'd rather be dead than cool" ("Stay Away"); "One more special message to go/And then I'm done then I can go home" ("On a Plain").

But as a man of riffs and letters, Cobain was a sly dog who rarely stooped to the obvious. He was a master of grim metaphor and droll sarcasm who delighted in shock treatment and false trails and then obliterated his tracks with industrial-strength guitar distortion and a corrosive whine 'n' bark that rubbed even his best hook lines raw. Nothing in Cobain's music was ever quite what it initially seemed; his best-known song was named after a deodorant. And he must have had a damn good laugh over all the critics — including this one — who tripped over that self-mocking opening couplet from "Serve the Servants": "Teenage angst has paid off well/Now I'm bored and old."

Because he wasn't bored. Not by music, anyway. In his suicide note, Cobain despaired that his muse had flown south for good. Yet even during those last black days, he refused to surrender without a fight: trying to record new Nirvana demos, initiating a project with R.E.M.'s Michael Stipe.

The blood, come, phlegm and venom splattered all over

Nirvana's albums, especially *In Utero*, were hard evidence of a young man torn by extremes — and still finding release, if not exactly sense or salvation, in the verse-chorus-verse fallout. Kurt Cobain made sure that if his life was going to end up on record, you got it as he fucking lived it.

I MISS THAT ALREADY. Cobain's music was a noise of purpose, not just vengeance, and rock & roll voices like his are not easy to replace. It was a noise of inclusion, too; when Cobain became successful, he dragged his peers and heroes — the Melvins, the Breeders, Meat Puppets, Half Japanese, the Raincoats — kicking and screaming into the spotlight. Cobain was also driven to find life beyond the punk-rock gravy train. MTV may have rerun Nirvana's *Unplugged* performance into the ground during that first weekend after Cobain's death, but the heavy rotation did not cheapen the promise and determination implicit in his dramatic acoustic recastings of "Come As You Are" and "Pennyroyal Tea."

Cobain's suicide is a defining moment in rock & roll for all the obvious reasons. As loath as he was to admit it, he was the first superstar of both the new punk and the new decade. He was also the first to check out permanently. Like the deaths of Jimi Hendrix, Janis Joplin, Elvis Presley and the other members of "that stupid club," as Cobain's mother uncharitably put it, his passing marked the end of an innocence — a greater communal euphoria that erupted when Nirvana's *Nevermind* tore a hole through the *Billboard* album chart at the end of 1991 and broke the death grip of mainstream-'80s pomp and bloat on rock & roll. For those three and four minutes apiece, "Smells Like Teen Spirit," "Come As You Are" and "Lithium" made commercial-rock radio sound alive, like a *weapon* again. Hearing those songs now, we can't help regretting how little Cobain shared in that euphoria.

The parallels between Cobain's life and that of John Lennon — who died when Cobain was only 13 — are downright spooky. Both came from broken homes, fought drug addiction, wrestled with the mixed blessings of success, entered into controversial, sometimes contentious marriages and carried the excess baggage from their troubled childhoods well past adolescence into adulthood. Like Lennon, whom he admired, Cobain spoke and wrote freely about his troubles and dreams without fear of ridicule or censure.

But Lennon was murdered; Cobain took his own life with a violent finality that ensured no turning back. Lennon, even during the most convulsive years of his career with and without the Beatles, reveled in the power of his celebrity, using it to press his own agenda. Cobain never figured out how to make stardom work for him.

After years of writing in bedrooms and playing in shitty little punk-rock bars, Cobain was blindsided when his music and his band suddenly became public domain. He saw "Smells Like Teen Spirit" — a song he'd written in blatant emulation of one of his favorite groups, Pixies — reduced to a cliché, the sing-along anthem of Flannel Nation. A line he'd written in dry jest, the kind of thing you'd say when you burst into a really boring party, became a slacker totem: "Here we are now, entertain us." By the start of Nirvana's 1993 fall tour, Cobain could barely bring himself to play the song with any enthusiasm. On the night of our interview at the Aragon Ballroom in Chicago, he didn't play it at all.

Yet rock & roll has always operated according to a premise of shared ownership – "Hey, baby, they're playing our song." Even Cobain was charged in the beginning by the need for belonging. He once remarked in a radio interview that the first song he ever learned to play was AC/DC's "Back in Black," arguably the definitive male-bonding headbanger of the early '80s.

"Smells Like Teen Spirit" is that kind of song, a lethal us-vs.-them blast of guitar crackle, strip-mined voice and brilliant reel-'em-in hooks ("Hello, hello, hello, *how low?*"). Let us also not forget how bassist Krist Novoselic and drummer Dave Grohl nailed that big-bang chorus to the floor. It only takes one song to define an epoch – or at least mark the starting line: "Heartbreak Hotel," "I Want to Hold Your Hand," "Like a Rolling Stone," "Anarchy in the U.K.," "The Message." "Teen Spirit" sent *Nevermind* into platinum orbit, broadcasting the dark side of the '80s Reagan-Bush gold rush – dysfunction, disenfranchisement, diminished expectations – with an almost contradictory vitality.

That was – and still is – the key to grunge: a music of black celebration rooted in the brutish white blooze of the early '70s, revved up with the chain-saw aggro of late-'70s punk and charged with an exorcising ferocity that is eternally teen-age and, when you get down to it, as old as the blues. The death, dope, sexual frustration and general ennui graphically documented in so much Seattle rock was real; so was the grasping for transcendence. The roaring hook line of Mudhoney's classic 1988 single "Touch Me I'm Sick" was like a badge of honor, a kind of radiant scar tissue. And when Pearl Jam played "Jeremy" – a song whose video is about teen suicide – in New York a week after Cobain's death, Eddie Vedder took pains to tell the audience that "living is the best revenge."

Frankly, if Cobain had never written and recorded another song as good as "Teen Spirit," his legacy would be secure. In fact, he left behind several that were even better, including "All Apologies" and "Pennyroyal Tea," from *In Utero*, and "About a Girl," a raw, droning beauty from Nirvana's 1989 debut album, *Bleach*. Underscoring the word games and thunder-crack riffs that cold-cocked young America in the punk-rock winter of '91-'92 was a depth of honesty, commitment and willing sacrifice that only a mosh-pit fuckwit could possibly miss.

If there is one line that sums up the power and candor of Kurt Cobain's genius (to hell with false modesty now), it's in the first verse of "Heart-Shaped Box": "I wish I could eat your cancer when you turn black," sung in a bruised but determined yelp over desultory strumming – just before the chorus blows your windows out. There's also the naked pleading of "Come As You Are" – note the extra, lamentory turnup in the word *memory* ("memor-e-e-*ah*") – and the low, throaty urgency of "Dumb," with its wounded-cello groan and striking image collision of lovesick prayer and drug communion ("My heart is broke/But I have some glue/Help me inhale/And mend it with you").

Never mind all the standard-issue babble about Generation X. There was nothing blank about the way Cobain articulated his broken dreams and wrapped up his discontent and, by extension, that of his audience, in roughshod song. When the shit hit the fans, they knew it for what it was – the plain truth.

GOING BY THE NUMBERS, Cobain didn't leave a lot of officially released music for us to obsess over: three Nirvana studio LPs, a catchall collection of the band's odds 'n' sods (1992's *Incesticide*) and enough leftovers – B sides, live tracks, BBC sessions, compilation tracks – to fill, at best, another album and a half. The essential facts of how Nirvana came together and managed to record Cobain's songs for posterity are also laughably out of proportion to the nuclear impact the band and its records had on young America.

Bleach, a potent document of Cobain's rapidly evolving songwriting, was recorded for $606.17 and sounds like it. The booming catharsis Nirvana aspired to onstage was funneled by Jack Endino's shoestring production into a gray, implosive roar that suited the abrupt, argumentative tenor of the songs. That is, with the notable exception of "About a Girl," whose roughly sketched Beatles-via-R.E.M. charm forecast Cobain's later stabs at scarred, low-volume balladry in "All Apologies" and *Nevermind*'s "Something in the Way."

Even *Nevermind* (exit drummer Chad Channing, enter Dave Grohl from the Washington, D.C., band Scream) was hardly an extravagance by the standards of most major labels. The total cost of the record was $135,000, including producer Butch Vig's fee (subsequently renegotiated). Still, Cobain later complained that he was "embarrassed" by the album's production, particularly the light-AOR-metal glaze that mixer Andy Wallace laid on the tracks (and which, no doubt, contributed to its massive sales). *Nevermind* was, Cobain said in Michael Azerrad's Nirvana biography, *Come As You Are*, "closer to a Mötley Crüe record than it is a punk-rock record." So much for the alternative revolution.

In Utero – plaintive, primal, petulant, pop-y, sometimes all at once – was the sum total of everything that went haywire in Cobain's life after *Nevermind*. The three-way fracas between Nirvana, the media and producer Steve Albini over whether Geffen would release the album (allegedly because of *In Utero*'s schizo, hard-sell personality) lasted longer than the actual recording sessions: a two-week blitz, with most of Cobain's vocals done in one day. The whole thing turned out to be a nonissue anyway: *In Utero* debuted at No. 1, and Nirvana embarked on their first full U.S. tour in almost two years, with Cobain declaring in these pages that "I've never been happier in my life."

I can't help thinking now that Cobain scammed me in our interview that night in Chicago. It was, he figured, something that his fans wanted to hear even if he didn't believe it. But I also can't help thinking that when he said it, at least he *wanted* to believe it, that he hadn't yet given up on finding a little nirvana of his own. More than anything else – the gigs, the videos, that interview – the image of Kurt Cobain that will stay etched in my mind is the sight of him at the *MTV Unplugged* taping, solo, bent over his acoustic guitar, pouring everything, the good, the bad, the ugly, into "Pennyroyal Tea." For at least those few minutes, he took on the demons by himself and won.

Rock & roll's finest moments inevitably come from its most troubled geniuses. Unfortunately, the troubled geniuses are the ones who find it the hardest to go the distance. May Kurt Cobain finally rest in peace. May we never forget how much we lost – and how much he gave up – to find it. ◑

By Donna Gaines

LIFE IN AMERICA can kill young people. Kurt Cobain was the Great White Hope for many kids trapped in bad lives. Growing up as an average teen in 1980s America, he shared a sad social history too common among members of his generation. A *lumpen-prole* hero, he not only made it out of teen-age wasteland alive, he soared to the highest ground. Cobain's triumph gave kids hope, faith that you could be yourself, be human and not get totally destroyed for it. He was the outcast kid's proof that in the end, truth would be revealed, and justice would prevail. In Nirvana, Cobain moved a kid's private hell to a generation's collective howl. He was not supposed to commit suicide.

In 1987, I investigated a teen-age suicide pact among four close friends who lived in a small, predominantly white, nonaffluent, suburban turnpike town. Like many places across America, Bergenfield, N.J., was economically depressed, offering limited opportunity to kids who didn't play the game. Like Cobain, the two boys and two girls were labeled as outcasts. Three out of the four came from families fractured by divorce; they all had lost loved ones suddenly and tragically. When things got too rough at home, the kids stayed with friends. The guys failed at several attempts at detox, rehab and recovery. Three of the four kids dropped out of high school and worked at dead-end jobs. They cherished their

friends, and they lived for rock & roll. In their collective suicide note, the four kids said they felt unloved. Like Cobain, they offered their love to anyone who would accept it.

Although girls attempt suicide with greater frequency, it is mainly a disease of white, nonurban males. Teen-age suicide was a virtually nonexistent category before 1960, but between 1950 and 1980 it nearly tripled. While America as a whole became less suicidal during the 1980s, people under 30 became dramatically more suicidal. While adolescents remain the most frequent attempters of suicide — an estimated 400,000 a year — the actual rates of suicide are higher once people enter their 20s. At the time of the Bergenfield suicide pact, suicide was the second leading killer of young people, after accidents, accounting for around 12 percent of youth mortalities. By the 1990s, suicide had been displaced by homicide. Today, suicide is the third leading method of destruction for young people. Firearms and alcohol are crucial elements in suicides.

The 1980s offered young people an experience of unsurpassed social violence and humiliation. Traumatized by absent or abusive parents, educators, police and shrinks, stuck in meaningless jobs without a livable wage, disoriented by disintegrating institutions, many kids felt trapped in a cycle of futility and despair. Adults fucked up across the board, abandoning an entire generation by failing to provide for or protect them or prepare them for independent living. Yet when young people began to exhibit symptoms of neglect, reflected in their rates of suicide, homicide, substance abuse, school failure, recklessness and general misery, adults condemned them as apathetic, illiterate, amoral losers.

Even the media couldn't resist capitalizing on "youth atrocities" — but we rarely bothered to ask the kids what was going on. When kids did seize the opportunity to speak, an existential terror too horrific to put into words was reduced to sound bites. Add to this the creepy litany of AIDS, global warming, unemployment and homelessness, and a gruesome landscape emerges. For more than a decade, taking on the brutality agenda — exposing the lies, fighting the bullshit — has been the central project of the Fucked Generation.

Throughout the worst years of our lives, the kids' music — hardcore, thrash metal and hip-hop — expressed the brutal truth of coming of age in Reagan's America. Since adults didn't get it, it was through the youth underground that kids created opportuni-

ties to explore the grim social realities they struggled against. Across music paradigms, artists as diverse as Slayer, N.W.A, Henry Rollins, Axl Rose, Suzanne Vega, Courtney Love and Morrissey have tried to work out this experience of humiliation and *abject*ification. By now, young people acknowledge alienation, deep loss and rage as normative conditions of living. To his credit, Kurt Cobain pushed the brutality agenda from the margins to the mainstream, disseminating it through mass culture like rapid fire.

Some kids don't make it out of high school alive. They give up before they even try. Others stick around, wounded, just to see what happens. Introverted and depressed, Cobain maybe was born with a morbid disposition. Maybe he had a chemical imbalance that made him too sensitive to live in the world, so that even true love, a beautiful daughter, a brilliant band, detox, family life and his wholesome Northwestern community rootedness couldn't fill the hole in his soul. At 27, Cobain was tired of being alive.

Maybe Cobain's anger and moral outrage kept him alive through his early, wasted years. Like most kids growing up in dying towns in dysfunctional-family situations, his expectations were pretty low. But the suicidal imagination has a dramatic flair. Like everyone with a rock & roll heart, he probably figured he would die young, go down in flames. He lived hard and fast, blew off school, relished his music, his friends, his recreational chemicals. If he didn't kill himself back then, it was probably because he had plans. He was busy painting, cutting demos, writing.

Many of the guys who live in white, nonaffluent dead-end towns from coast to coast grow up feeling they're gonna die young. When some guys I know heard about Cobain, they made note of his age – the dreaded age of rocker mortality, when Jimi, Janis and Jim crash-burned from too much too soon. For the average 27-year-old, though, life today isn't so glamorous. They're struggling with rent, health insurance and car payments. But their dreams haven't died. They're still playing music, making plans and working hard. Bands rehearse, lovers fantasize about weddings, kids, a nice place to live. They strive for serenity and sobriety. To keep life simple and honest, to live decently. Friends huddle together, helping each other, and little by little, they keep moving forward.

Kurt Cobain and Courtney Love knew they had problems. They understood themselves as unloved children, as co-dependents. They took turns rescuing and protecting each other from exploitation, illness, bad publicity. They said they wanted a better emotional life for their daughter, Frances Bean; they wanted her to feel loved.

I remember reading how Love held Cobain's hand, soothing him through his heroin withdrawal in the delivery room while she was giving birth to their child. She once said all she wanted was to make Cobain happy. The same week all her rocker dreams came true, Mrs. Kurt Cobain was again preoccupied with her husband's needs. After he died, she said she didn't know what more she could have done to help him. Nothing worked: not true love, not tough love, not Frances Bean, detox, rehab, therapy or prayer. Nothing Love could have done would have prevented Cobain's suicide. No one person can be an ongoing life-support system for another.

Yet some people blame Love for destroying Cobain. Others blame the media for crucifying the couple, or the state (child-welfare authorities, for example) for labeling them unfit parents and

unnecessarily worrying them again about losing their daughter. Was it pressure from the band, the biz, the jolting anomie of massive fame? The drugs, the chronic stomach pain? Was Cobain a gifted, troubled soul whose misery was so deep that nothing would ever make him happy? No matter how far we travel in life, are we always at risk of feeling worthless, hopeless and helpless?

We've heard endless public discussion about the low self-esteem suffered by young Americans, the supposed root of all the self-destructive "acting out" behaviors. An entire generation of de facto abused and neglected children has been remanded to psychotherapy to cure the results of a collapsed social order. Young people resisted this panacea with a keen political instinct, viewing shrink-o-rama as just one more fixture on the brutality landscape. The anarchist's soul will resist normative proscriptives for daily living as social control. Despite the genuine intentions of an army of helping professionals, many young people would just rather have a beer and talk things over with a friend.

"I STILL CAN'T GET OVER the frustration, the guilt and the empathy I have for everyone. There's good in all of us, and I simply think I love people too much, so much that it makes me feel too fucking sad. . . . I love and feel sorry for people too much." In her widow's wail, as Love read portions of Cobain's suicide note at the Seattle Center, she challenged him: If he loved everyone so much, why the *hell* didn't he just stick around?

Kurt Cobain was a Pisces, the sign known as the dustbin of the zodiac. That made him a psychic sponge for collective feelings, able to intuit and absorb everything around him. With the archetype of Jesus Christ, we ushered in the Piscean Age, whose attributes are self-sacrifice, surrender and martyrdom. According to lore, the Pisces would rather self-destruct than cause harm to others, in effect, is willing to die for the sins of others. There is a dark side to Pisces that can motivate self-pity, defeatism, alcoholism and suicide. The Pisces soul is tender and has difficulty filtering out the negative. Most Pisceans waver between extremes. Apparently, Cobain had an affinity for Jesus. Maybe he had a martyr complex and saw himself as a humble servant who absorbed our human pain, even against his own will. Cobain's "burning, nauseous stomach" was his bleeding heart.

In his way, Kurt Cobain tried to show us how to live – he prayed for the racist, the homophobe, the misogynist. But he wasn't Jesus, and he couldn't save us. Despite his compassion, he wasn't an altruist who died for anybody's sins. His suicide was a betrayal; it negated an unspoken contract among members of a generation who depended on one another to reverse the parental generation's legacy of neglect, confusion and frustration. Cobain broke that promise. He just walked.

From Jesus to Cobain in 2,000 years. There's no Mommy or Daddy, no great savior coming down to walk us through the millennium. As the Aquarian Age seeps into our collective consciousness, we'll need to be a nation of messiahs, individuals working together, looking out for one another. The Fucked Generation has already figured that out. It's been doing it for years. ◐

"Remember Kurt for what he was: caring, generous, and sweet. Let's keep the music with us. We'll always have it, forever." --- Krist Novoselic

IT'S NO COINCIDENCE that Kurt Cobain was obsessed with Leadbelly, the legendary bluesman. Cobain, too, had a gift for encapsulating his daily concerns in a few deceptively simple lyrics, then energizing those sentiments with memorable melodies and an inimitable delivery. "School," as genius a song as Nirvana ever produced, universalizes the rage and frustration every person experiences going through life adjudged by social cliques ("No recess!") in a mere 15 words.

"Love Buzz," Nirvana's first single — a psychedelic love song originally recorded by the obscure '70s Swedish group Shocking Blue — lacks the canny mix of experimentalism and accessibility that brands the band's own best work. "Big Cheese," the single's B side, hits closer to the mark; from its abstract, plodding chord progression to the mocking humor of its lyrics (ostensibly about Sub Pop head Jonathan Poneman), it rips and roars its way into a gnarled piece of genuine punk art. While other early tracks, such as "Hairspray Queen," "Beeswax" and "Mexican Seafood" (available on the 1992 DGC collection *Incesticide*), each contain shards of compositional brilliance — and hint at influences ranging from Gang of Four to Sonic Youth — Cobain had yet to hit upon "the voice," a magnificent instrument that could carry a tune even at full scream.

Considering its tiny recording budget, Nirvana's 1989 debut album, *Bleach* (Sub Pop), comes off like the world's most astonishing field recording. Despite the occasional rushed take or muddied mix, the songs and arrangements are wholly formed. On heavy-metalish tracks such as "Paper Cuts" and "Negative Creep," one hears Cobain twist and strain his voice to mimic the pain that accompanies, respectively, being abused as a child and being ostracized as an adolescent. But it's the songs with the carefully devised melodies, "About a Girl," "School" and "Scoff," that bulge with the promise of mass appeal. Not a note is wasted: Witness "Swap Meet," a claustrophobic snapshot of rural America's desperate flea-market culture, amid which Cobain carves out an elegant, inventive guitar solo where others would have opted for throwaway noise.

For past generations, rock & roll signified liberation, freedom from the ordinary world and its expectations; but in Cobain's case, rock equaled enslavement. On one hand, it had served as the perfect release from the truncated existence he suffered — like so many other small-town teens — growing up. On the other, Cobain learned quicker than most that dedicating oneself wholeheartedly to perpetuating punk's rock-till-you-drop mythos has become a creative dead end. "Blew," *Bleach*'s claustrophobic lead-off track, acknowledges musically that microcosm's low ceiling; Krist Novoselic's nimble, rumbling bass line is all that keeps the punch-drunk melody from taking a spill. Add lyrics such as "If you wouldn't mind, I would like to breathe," and *Bleach*'s status as the ultimate high school anti-party LP is secure.

The *Blew* EP (Tupelo, U.K., 1989) adds "Stain" and "Been a Son," tangible proof of the performance chemistry developing between Cobain and Novoselic. On "Been a Son," particularly, the guitar and bass wend their furious path together, generating a pop

energy slowed only by Chad Channing's perfunctory drumming. "Sliver," the next single for Sub Pop, written with Mudhoney drummer Dan Peters, was the first generous glimpse of the band's knack for melding Beatlesque melodies with a brisk, noise-tinged groove.

The band's concern that it sounded too slick notwithstanding, 1991's *Nevermind* (DGC) is Nirvana's stylistic breakthrough — a masterwork. The additions of Dave Grohl, the rare drummer who can pound and swing simultaneously, and producer Butch Vig somehow galvanized a revolutionary sound. (Grohl's rapid-fire attacks on "Breed" and "Territorial Pissings" are evidence alone that Nirvana had settled upon its optimum lineup.) And the lyrics are remarkably coherent, considering Cobain's tendency to slight their significance. By isolating and heightening each musical element in its repertoire — from the way the chorus kicks into overdrive on "Smells Like Teen Spirit" to the multitextured guitar parts on "Polly" and "Lithium" to the delicately whispered vocal on "Something in the Way" — Nirvana and Vig proved that raw, punk-inspired rock could have a lush grandeur all its own.

Nevermind is a discourse on the erotic lure of the profane, related in the most forthright, unprofaned terms possible. On "Drain You," two infants mewl and puke their way through the finer points of baby politics; on "Come As You Are," Cobain welcomes old enemies with the oddly censorious "And I swear that I don't have a gun." The songs "Stay Away," "On a Plain" and "Something in the Way" form a trilogy about a soul in retreat: The first lashes out at the cool patrol; the second rivals the Who's "The Real Me" as a mythic tale of adolescent insolubility; the third finds that same soul, spent and splattered in bodily fluids. "But it's OK to eat fish," moans Cobain, a Pisces. " 'Cause they haven't any feelings."

The sprinkling of extra tracks that filled subsequent single releases are of comparable quality. The "Smells Like Teen Spirit" single, specifically, is a must-have for the pure-punk "Even in His Youth" and the quintessential rendering of "Aneurysm" — Nirvana's ingeniously deflated history of rock, from "The Twist" to arena rock, via Johnny Rotten.

In Utero (DGC, 1993) reads like a map on which all trails lead back to the womb, a prelude to *Nevermind*. The concentric cries of "Heart-Shaped Box" — from fetus, heart and locked closet — link infantilism and adulthood as brilliantly as any in rock's history. Critics might credibly contend that too many of *In Utero*'s songs whine about the fury fame hath wrought (the jaded lyrics of the otherwise powerful "Serve the Servants" could accompany the music of a hundred and one dinosaur bands), but at its best, *In Utero* transcends circumstance.

In retrospect, one of *In Utero*'s most startling revelations is the maturation of one of rock's great trios. "Scentless Apprentice" finds Novoselic deftly scaling his fretboard alongside Grohl's raunchy Zeppelin-esque beat, freeing Cobain to dapple the musical canvas with stunning gales of noise. His vocals, too, are wonderfully stylized, occasionally slurred or delivered in a fake English accent. "Dumb" could be a midcareer Beatles hit, albeit tanked up on codeine.

139

Sure, it's tempting to presage Cobain's suicide in the necrophilic lyrics of "Milk It," though heavy-metal homage is a better guess. But don't try chalking up the unadulterated bile of "Rape Me" to pretense; Cobain's chillingly screamed coda is so candid that it's downright embarrassing: Listeners can't help but be disarmed by the sheer nakedness of Cobain's emotional display.

"Verse Chorus Verse," an *In Utero* outtake available (uncredited) on Arista's 1993 *No Alternative* benefit album, belies its perfunctory title with a hauntingly original melody. The arch "I Hate Myself and I Want to Die" – strangely misplaced on Geffen's 1994 *The Beavis and Butt-head Experience* compilation – reveals a looser, more swaggering Nirvana hitting a rather astonishing new stride.

In November 1992, Cobain laid down a guitar track to accompany William S. Burroughs' reading, *The "Priest" They Called Him* (Tim Kerr). The nine-minute tale of a junkie clergyman who administers himself the "immaculate fix," it's a religion-as-drug analogy as affecting as it is clichéd. Perhaps a fitting farewell to a band that outwardly came to embody the very rock traditions it once railed against, even as it jetted a screaming rocket to the future whose smoldering fuselage will bear examining by music fans well into the next century. ◐

Disco

U.S. Singles and EPs

These are vinyl only, excluding the DGC releases, which are CD singles.

"Love Buzz"/"Big Cheese"
SUB POP, 1988

"Mexican Seafood"
on *Teriyaki Asthma Vol. I*
C/Z, 1989

"Sliver"/"Dive"
SUB POP, 1990

"Molly's Lips" by Nirvana/"Candy" by the Fluid
SUB POP, 1991

"Here She Comes Now" by Nirvana/
"Venus in Furs" by the Melvins
COMMUNION, 1991

"Smells Like Teen Spirit"/
"Even in His Youth"/"Aneurysm"
DGC, 1991

"Come As You Are"/"School" (live)/"Drain You" (live)
DGC, 1992

"Lithium"/"Been a Son" (live)/"Curmudgeon"
DGC, 1992

"Puss" by Jesus Lizard/
"Oh, the Guilt" by Nirvana
TOUCH AND GO, 1993

THE MELVINS & BUZZO

Dale Crover

U.S. Albums (CDs)

Bleach
SUB POP, 1989

Blew
Floyd the Barber
About a Girl
School
Love Buzz
Paper Cuts
Negative Creep
Scoff
Swap Meet
Mr. Moustache
Sifting
Big Cheese
Downer

Nevermind
DGC, 1991

Smells Like Teen Spirit
In Bloom
Come As You Are
Breed
Lithium
Polly
Territorial Pissings
Drain You
Lounge Act
Stay Away
On a Plain
Something in the Way
Endless, Nameless (uncredited)

Incesticide
DGC, 1992

Dive
Sliver
Stain
Been a Son
Turnaround
Molly's Lips
Son of a Gun
(New Wave) Polly
Beeswax
Downer
Mexican Seafood
Hairspray Queen
Aero Zeppelin
Big Long Now
Aneurysm

In Utero
DGC, 1993

Serve the Servants
Scentless Apprentice
Heart-Shaped Box
Rape Me
Frances Farmer Will Have Her
	Revenge on Seattle
Dumb
Very Ape
Milk It
Pennyroyal Tea
Radio Friendly Unit Shifter
Tourette's
All Apologies

Songs on Compilations

"Spank Thru"
on *Sub Pop 200*
SUB POP, 1988

"Do You Love Me"
on *Hard to Believe*
(Kiss tribute album)
C/Z, 1990

"Dive"
on *The Grunge Years*
SUB POP, 1991

"Beeswax"
on *Kill Rock Stars*
KILL ROCK STARS, 1991

"Mexican Seafood"
on *Teriyaki Asthma Vol. I–V*
C/Z, 1991

"Here She Comes Now"
on *Heaven and Hell, Vol. 1*
(Velvet Underground
tribute album)
COMMUNION, 1991

"Return of the Rat"
on *Eight Songs for
Greg Sage*
TIM KERR, 1992

"Return of the Rat"
on *Fourteen Songs for
Greg Sage & the Wipers*
TIM KERR, 1993

"Verse Chorus Verse"
(uncredited) on *No Alternative*
ARISTA, 1993

"I Hate Myself and
I Want To Die"
on *The Beavis and
Butt-head Experience*
GEFFEN, 1993

"Pay to Play"
on *DGC Rarities Vol. 1*
DGC, 1994

Other Kurt Cobain Appearances

Bikini Twilight
by Go Team,
featuring Cobain
K, 1989

"Where Did You Sleep Last
Night?"
on *The Winding Sheet* by
Mark Lanegan,
featuring Cobain on guitar
and Krist Novoselic on bass
SUB POP, 1990

Bureaucratic Desire for Revenge
(EP) by Earth,
featuring Cobain
SUB POP, 1991

The "Priest" They Called Him
by William Burroughs
spoken word, featuring
Cobain on guitar
TIM KERR, 1993

Houdini
by the Melvins, with Cobain
as one of the producers
ATLANTIC, 1993

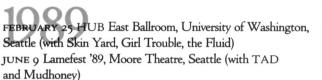

Selective Tourography

1988
JANUARY 23 Community World Theatre, Tacoma, WA (under the name Ted Ed Fred)
MARCH 19 Community World Theatre, Tacoma, WA (with Lush)
JULY 3 The Vogue, Seattle (with Blood Circus)
OCTOBER 30 Dorm party at Evergreen State College, Olympia, WA (first time band trashes equipment, begins with Kurt smashing guitar)

1989
FEBRUARY 25 HUB East Ballroom, University of Washington, Seattle (with Skin Yard, Girl Trouble, the Fluid)
JUNE 9 Lamefest '89, Moore Theatre, Seattle (with TAD and Mudhoney)
JUNE 22 Covered Wagon, San Francisco (begin 26-date, first extensive U.S. tour)
JULY 9 Sonic Temple, Pittsburgh, PA
JULY 18 Pyramid Club, New York City (New Music Seminar)
OCTOBER 20 Newcastle, England (with TAD, begin first European tour, 36 shows in 42 days)
DECEMBER 3 The Astoria, London, England (last tour date, with TAD and Mudhoney)
DECEMBER 28 The Underground, Seattle (release party for Sub Pop's *Sub Pop 200*)

1990
APRIL 1 Cabaret Metro, Chicago (begin 15-date U.S./Canadian tour)
MAY 17 The Zoo, Boise, ID (last date on tour)
AUGUST 23 Melody Ballroom, Portland, OR (opening for Sonic Youth)
AUGUST 24 Moore Theatre, Seattle (opening for Sonic Youth)
SEPTEMBER 22 Motor Sports International and Garage, Seattle (with Melvins, Dwarves, Derelicts; crowd of 1,500 was Nirvana's biggest audience to date)

1991
MARCH 5 The Bronx, Edmonton, Canada (first of 3 Canadian dates)
JUNE 14 Hollywood Palladium, Hollywood, CA (with Hole, opening for Dinosaur Jr)
JUNE 15 Iguana's, Tijuana, Mexico (opening for Dinosaur Jr)
AUGUST 15 The Roxy, Los Angeles (with Wool)
AUGUST 20 Sir Henry's, Cork, Ireland (begin U.K./European tour with Sonic Youth, Dinosaur Jr, Mudhoney, Smashing Pumpkins)
SEPTEMBER 1 Rotterdam De Doelen, Rotterdam, Netherlands (last date of 9-date tour)
SEPTEMBER 20 Opera House, Toronto, Canada (begin extensive North American *Nevermind* tour)
SEPTEMBER 28 The Marquee, New York City (the Melvins open)
OCTOBER 4 Cat's Cradle, Chapel Hill, NC (Das Damen opens)
OCTOBER 14 First Avenue, Minneapolis (Urge Overkill opens)
OCTOBER 27 The Palace, Hollywood, CA (Hole and Greg Sage open)

OCTOBER 31 Paramount Theatre, Seattle (last date of 31-date tour; Mudhoney, Bikini Kill open)
NOVEMBER 4 Bierkeller, Bristol, England (first date of 6-week U.K./European tour)
DECEMBER 27 Sports Arena, Los Angeles (with Pearl Jam, open for Red Hot Chili Peppers)
DECEMBER 31 Cow Palace, San Francisco (with Pearl Jam and Red Hot Chili Peppers)

1992

JANUARY 11 *Saturday Night Live,* New York City
JANUARY 24 Phoenician Club, Sydney, Australia (begin 6-week tour of Australia, New Zealand, Japan)
FEBUARY 14 Kokusai Koryu Center, Osaka, Japan (first Japanese show)
FEBRUARY 21 Pink's Garage, Honolulu, HI (first of two shows in Hawaii)
JUNE 21 The Point, Dublin, Ireland (first of 10 dates in Europe)
AUGUST 22 County Fairgrounds, Portland, OR
AUGUST 23 Seattle Center Coliseum, Seattle

1993

JANUARY 16 Murumbi Stadium, Sao Paulo, Brazil (L7 opens)
JANUARY 23 Praca Da Apotoese, Rio de Janiero, Brazil (L7 opens)
APRIL 9 Cow Palace, San Francisco (with L7, Breeders, Disposable Heroes of Hiphoprisy; Bosnian Rape Victims Benefit)
JULY 23 Roseland Ballroom, New York City (Jesus Lizard opens, New Music Seminar)
OCTOBER 2 Finsbury Park, London, England
OCTOBER 18 Arizona State Fair, Phoenix, AZ (kicks off 45-date U.S. tour)
OCTOBER 30 Hara Arena, Dayton, OH (Meat Puppets, the Boredoms open)
NOVEMBER 7 William and Mary Hall, Williamsburg, VA (the Breeders, Half Japanese open)
NOVEMBER 27 Bayfront Park & Amphitheatre, Miami, FL (Come, the Breeders open)
DECEMBER 10 The Forum, St. Paul, MN (the Breeders, Shonen Knife open)
DECEMBER 30 The Great Western Forum, Inglewood, CA (Butthole Surfers, Chokebore open)

1994

JANUARY 1 Jackson County Expo Hall, Medford, OR (with Butthole Surfers, Chokebore)
JANUARY 6 Spokane Coliseum, Spokane, WA (the Breeders open)
JANUARY 7 Seattle Center Arena (first of 2 shows, with the Breeders, Chokebore)
JANUARY 8 Seattle Center Arena (Nirvana's final U.S. show)
FEBRUARY 6 Pavilhao Carlos Lopes, Lisbon, Portugal (first show of European tour)
MARCH 1 Terminal Einz, Munich, Germany (Nirvana's final performance)

Grant Alden was managing editor of *The Rocket* magazine in Seattle from March 1989 to March 1994. At present he is a freelance writer and co-owner of Vox Populi Gallery.

Lorraine Ali is a Los Angeles–based writer whose work has appeared in ROLLING STONE and various other publications, including the *Los Angeles Times* and *Option* magazine.

Michael Azerrad, a former ROLLING STONE contributing editor, is the author of *Come As You Are: The Story of Nirvana.* His two-year association with Nirvana revived his faith in rock music and profoundly changed his life.

Anthony DeCurtis is a writer and editor at ROLLING STONE, where he oversees the record-review section. He is the editor of *Present Tense: Rock & Roll and Culture* and co-editor of *The* ROLLING STONE *Illustrated History of Rock & Roll* and *The* ROLLING STONE *Album Guide.* He won a Grammy for his liner notes for the Eric Clapton retrospective *Crossroads* and has twice won the ASCAP Deems Taylor Award for excellence in writing about music. He holds a Ph.D. in American literature from Indiana University and lectures frequently on cultural matters.

Alec Foege is the author of *Confusion Is Next: The Sonic Youth Story.* A regular contributor to ROLLING STONE and various other publications, he was formerly a senior editor and is currently a contributing editor at *Spin.*

David Fricke is the music editor of ROLLING STONE and has written for the magazine since 1979. He is also the American correspondent for the British weekly *Melody Maker.* He is the author of *Animal Instinct,* a biography of Def Leppard, and has written liner notes for major retrospective CD collections by the Byrds, Led Zeppelin, John Prine, Hüsker Dü and his favorite band of all time — Moby Grape.

Dr. Donna Gaines is a sociologist and journalist. She is the author of *Teenage Wasteland: Suburbia's Dead End Kids.*

Mikal Gilmore is a ROLLING STONE contributing editor and the author of *Shot in the Heart.*

Greil Marcus is a ROLLING STONE contributing editor. His books include *Mystery Train, Lipstick Traces, Dead Elvis* and *Ranters & Crowd Pleasers.*

Chris Mundy is a senior writer at ROLLING STONE and was a co-producer of the 1993 AIDS benefit album *No Alternative.*

Kim Neely is a ROLLING STONE contributing editor.

Ann Powers is a senior editor at the *Village Voice* and has written for ROLLING STONE, the *New York Times* and various other publications. She is co-editor with Evelyn McDonnell of *She Said, She Said: Women Writing About Rock, Pop, and Rap.*

Ira Robbins is the pop music critic of *New York Newsday* and the editor of *The Trouser Press Record Guide.*

Neil Strauss writes for ROLLING STONE, the *New York Times* and the *Village Voice,* among other publications. He compiled and edited *Radiotext(e),* an anthology of radio-related writings.

Picture Credits

Art Rock p. 46

Jim Berry p. 113, 114

Michael Blackburn p. 111

Lee Bolton p. 45

Julian Broad p. 26-27, 28, 31

Calef Brown p. 55

Philip Burke p. 62-63, back cover

Anton Corbijn p. 124-125

Chris Cuffaro/ Outline Press p. 49, 53

Jesse Frohman/ Outline Press p. 70

Courtesy Geffen Records p. 139

Guzman p. 9, 10, 11, 12-13, 14, 73

Frank Kozik p. 43

Jeff Kravitz p. 102-103

Brian Krueger p. 50-51

M. Linssen/Redferns/ Retna Pictures p. 60

Tracy Marander p. 16-17, 18 (upper left, middle, lower left), 116

Frank Micelotta/ Outline Press p. 135, 136-137

Charles Peterson/Retna Pictures p. 80-81, 95

Steve Pyke/Retna Pictures p. 56-57, 59

Tom Reese/Seattle Times/Sipa Press p. 88-89

James Rexroad/Sipa Press p. 92-93

Seattle Post Intelligencer/Sygma p. 109

Mark Seliger cover, p. 32, 36, 37, 67, 97

Sestini Agency/Gamma Liaison p. 84-85

Ed Sirrs/Retna Pictures p. 79

Juergen Teller/ Outline Press p. 120, 121, 122, 123

Jeffrey Thurnher/ Outline Press p. 76

Ian Tilton/ Retna Pictures p. 18 (upper right)

John Troutman Collection p. 140, 141

Esther Watson p. 144

Kirk Weddle p. 20-21

Kirk Weddle/ Sipa Press p. 22-23, 24-25

Alice Wheeler p. 18 (bottom right), 98-99

Dan Winters p. 112, 129, 130, 131, 133

A NUMBER OF PEOPLE worked very hard to make this book possible. Many thanks to all the writers and editors of ROLLING STONE whose endeavors are showcased here, as well as ROLLING STONE's Jann S. Wenner, Kent Brownridge, John Lagana, Fred Woodward, Denise Sfraga, Sid Holt, Barbara O'Dair, Bill Van Parys, Jodi Peckman, Gail Anderson, Debra Bishop Henderson, Geraldine Hessler, Lee Bearson, Tobias Perse, Kevin Mullan, Willis Caster, Eric Flaum and Elsie St. Leger. We'd also like to thank our editor at Little, Brown, Michael Pietsch, and our literary agent Sarah Lazin.

In addition, thanks go to Fredrik Sundwall, Stacia Sobieski, Jim Merlis, Sheenah Fair, Simon Fair Timony, Alex Macleod, Janet Billig, John Silva, Sidney Painter, Carrie Smith, Anthony Bozza, Sheryl Olson, Walter Armstrong, Nancy Bilyeau, Yoomi Chong, Jacki Bookshester, Patricia Day Cobb, Jay Smith and Michael Meisel.

Our gratitude, too, to the artists and photographers whose work is pictured here as well as to those who provided us with their memorabilia: John Troutman, Tracy Marander, Kevin Plamondon at Art Rock and Grant Alden at Vox Populi Gallery. The Fell Types used in this book were rendered digitally by Jonathan Hoeffler.

Of course, most of all, we thank Kurt Cobain, Krist Novoselic and Dave Grohl for making music that has enriched our lives.

Holly George-Warren & Shawn Dahl
Editors, Rolling Stone Press
July 1994

ed from Nirvana. August 1990 Nirvana opens for Sonic Youth on a West Coast tour. Grover sits in on drums. Sept. 22, 1990 Nirvana plays the Motor Sports International and Garage with Mudhoney's Dan Peters on drums. Peters gets the boot a few days afterward. Sept. 25, 1990 David Grohl of the freshly defunct Washington, D.C., hardcore band Scream joins Nirvana. October 1990 Nirvana tours briefly in England with L7. April 30, 1991 After a fervid bidding war, Nirvana signs with Geffen/DGC Records. May-June 1991 Nirvana records their major-label debut, "Nevermind," with producer Butch Vig. June 1991 They briefly tour the U.S., opening for Dinosaur Jr. August 1991 Nirvana opens for Sonic Youth on a European festival tour, including a landmark performance at the Reading Festival. Sept. 20, 1991 Nirvana kicks off a six-week U.S. tour. Sept. 24, 1991 "Nevermind" is released; 46,251 copies shipped across the U.S. Oct. 12, 1991 "Nevermind" debuts on the "Billboard" albums chart at No. 144. Oct. 29, 1991 "Nevermind" goes gold. Nov. 2, 1991 The band begins a six-week European tour as "Nirvanamania" sweeps the U.S. MTV plays the "Smells Like Teen Spirit" video constantly, and the song is hailed as the anthem for a generation. November 1991 "Nevermind" goes platinum. December 1991 Nirvana does a quick U.S. tour with Pearl Jam and the Red Hot Chili Peppers. Jan. 11, 1992 "Nevermind" hits No. 1 the "Billboard" albums chart. The same day, Nirvana plays "Saturday Night Live." January-February 1992 Nirvana tours Australia, New Zealand, Japan and Hawaii. Feb. 4, 1992 "Nevermind" goes to No. 1 again. Feb. 24, 1992 Cobain and Hole leader Courtney Love are married in Hawaii. June-early July 1992 Nirvana tours Europe. August 1992 Lynn Hirschberg reports in "Vanity Fair" that Love used heroin during her pregnancy. Aug. 18, 1992 Frances Bean Cobain is born. Children's Services of Los Angeles County immediately revokes custody of the child, a direct result of